SAINTS OF THE LITURGICAL YEAR: BRIEF BIOGRAPHIES

Joseph N. Tylenda, S.J.

Georgetown University Press, Washington, D.C.

Library of Congress Cataloging-in-Publication Data

Saints of the liturgical year / compiled by Joseph N. Tylenda.
    p.   cm.
   ISBN 0-87840-498-8 : $5.95
   1. Christian saints--Biography.   2. Church year--Prayer-books and
devotions--English.   3. Catholic Church--Prayer-books and devotions-
-English.   4. Christian saints--Prayer-books and devotions--English.
I. Tylenda, Joseph N.
BX4655.2.S243   1989
282'.092'2--dc20
[B]   89-27158
                                           CIP

Contents

Leo Mangin, priest, and companions, martyrs, *Memorial*
5   Agatha, virgin and martyr, *Memorial*
6   Paul Miki, religious, and companions, martyrs, *Memorial*
8   Jerome Emiliani, priest
10 Scholastica, virgin, *Memorial*
11 Our Lady of Lourdes
14 Cyril, monk, and Methodius, bishop, *Memorial*
15 Claude La Colombière, priest
17 Seven Founders of the Order of Servites
21 Peter Damian, bishop and doctor
22 Chair of St. Peter, apostle, *Feast*
23 Polycarp, bishop and martyr, *Memorial*

March   28
3   Katharine Drexel, virgin
4   Casimir
7   Perpetua and Felicity, martyrs, *Memorial*
8   John of God, religious
9   Frances of Rome, religious
17 Patrick, bishop
18 Cyril of Jerusalem, bishop and doctor
19 Joseph, husband of Mary, *Solemnity*
23 Turibius of Mogrovejo, bishop
25 Annunciation of the Lord, *Solemnity*

April   35
2   Francis of Paola, hermit
4   Isidore, bishop and doctor
5   Vincent Ferrer, priest
7   John Baptist de la Salle, priest, *Memorial*
11 Stanislaus, bishop and martyr, *Memorial*
13 Martin I, pope and martyr
21 Anselm, bishop and doctor
22 Blessed Virgin Mary, Mother of the Society of Jesus, *Feast*

6   Norbert, bishop
9   Joseph de Anchieta, priest
     Ephrem, deacon and doctor
11 Barnabas, apostle, *Memorial*
13 Anthony of Padua, priest and doctor, *Memorial*
19 Romuald, abbot
21 Aloysius Gonzaga, religious, *Memorial*
22 Paulinus of Nola, bishop
     John Fisher, bishop and martyr and Thomas
       More, martyr
24 Birth of St. John the Baptist, *Solemnity*
27 Cyril of Alexandria, bishop and doctor
28 Irenaeus, bishop and martyr, *Memorial*
29 Peter and Paul, apostles, *Solemnity*
30 First Martyrs of the Church of Rome

July   77

2   Bernardine Realino, John Francis Regis, Francis
     Jerome, Julian Maunoir and Anthony Baldinucci,
     priests, *Memorial*
3   Thomas, apostle, *Feast*
4   Elizabeth of Portugal
5   Anthony Zaccaria, priest
6   Maria Goretti, virgin and martyr
11 Benedict, abbot, *Memorial*
13 Henry
14 Kateri Tekakwitha, virgin, *Memorial*
     Camillus de Lellis, priest
15 Bonaventure, bishop and doctor, *Memorial*
16 Our Lady of Mount Carmel
21 Lawrence of Brindisi, priest and doctor
22 Mary Magdalene, *Memorial*
23 Bridget, religious
25 James, apostle, *Feast*
26 Joachim and Ann, parents of Mary, *Memorial*
29 Martha, *Memorial*
30 Peter Chrysologus, bishop and doctor

9   Peter Claver, priest, *Memorial*
10 Francis Gárate, religious
13 John Chrysostom, bishop and doctor, *Memorial*
14 Triumph of the Cross, *Feast*
15 Our Lady of Sorrows, *Memorial*
16 Cornelius, pope and martyr, and Cyprian,
      bishop and martyr, *Memorial*
17 Robert Bellarmine, bishop and doctor, *Memorial*
19 Januarius, bishop and martyr
20 Andrew Kim Taegon, Paul Chong and companions,
      martyrs, *Memorial*
21 Matthew, apostle and evangelist, *Feast*
26 Cosmas and Damian, martyrs
27 Vincent de Paul, priest, *Memorial*
28 Wenceslaus, martyr
    Lawrence Ruiz and companions, martyrs
29 Michael, Gabriel, and Raphael, archangels, *Feast*
30 Jerome, priest and doctor, *Memorial*

October   131

1   Theresa of the Child Jesus, virgin, *Memorial*
2   Guardian angels, *Memorial*
3   Francis Borgia, priest, *Memorial*
4   Francis of Assisi, *Memorial*
6   Diego Aloysius de San Vitores, priest and martyr
    Bruno, priest
    Rose-Marie Durocher, virgin
7   Our Lady of the Rosary, *Memorial*
9   Denis, bishop and martyr, and companions, martyrs
    John Leonardi, priest
14 John Ogilvie, priest and martyr, *Memorial*
    Callistus I, pope and martyr
15 Teresa of Jesus, virgin, *Memorial*
16 Hedwig, religious
    Margaret Mary Alacoque, virgin
17 Ignatius of Antioch, bishop and martyr, *Memorial*
18 Luke, evangelist, *Feast*

Introduction

After a decade-long slump in interest from the late 60s through the middle 70s, the Saints have begun to recapture the minds and hearts of Roman Catholics as a sources of inspiration and encouragement. Collections of biographical essays, like *Saints for All Seasons*, full length biographies of popular Saints like Francis of Assisi, Theresa of Lisieux, Ignatius of Loyola, and of more contemporary religious figures like Thomas Merton and Mother Teresa have also been published with both critical and popular acclaim. This revival of interests, however, runs parallel with a large amount of ignorance about the lives of the Saints, especially among Catholics who grew up during the period of their virtual eclipse in catechetical and liturgical instruction.

This convenient handbook should help to remedy that situation, at least in so far as the Saints of the liturgical calendar are concerned. Organized according to the memorials and feast days of the liturgical year*, it provides a brief biography of each of the Saints commemorated in the Mass, giving the kind of information that would be of most use for celebtrants who wish to say a few words about the Saint of the day at the beginning of Mass, or who might want to point out in their homilies how the life of the Saint is reflected in special readings chosen for the day's Mass formulary. The aim is to be succinct and informative about the events of the Saint's life, leaving the celebrant or homilist free to develop whatever themes seem more appropriate.

Certainly, teachers in Caholic schools or in CCD programs will find the same information helpful for introducing students to the history of the Church as it has been exemplified by her heroes and heroines. The mystery of the Church is most fully alive and most approachable through these remarkable individuals; connecting their stories with the central story of Christ's Paschal mystery will enliven and deepen catechetical instruction.

Finally, many Catholics who attend Mass regularly during the week no longer own a missal since the use of the vernacular has made the prayers and readings readily intelligible. One result is that even the quite brief sketches of the life of the Saint of the day which appear in the daily missal are no longer available. The biographical sketches here are considerabnly more detailed and informative, but are still brief enough to be looked at five or ten minutes before leaving for Mass. The book is designed to fit handily on the shelf alongside the Bible, the Sunday Missal, and other reading.

Note

Saints of the Liturgical Year is based upon the *General Roman Calendar*, presently in use in the Roman Catholic Church, together with the *Proper Calendar for the Dioceses of the United States of America* as decreed by the Bishops' Committee on the Liturgy of the National Conference of Catholic Bishops, and the *General Liturgical Calendar of the Society of Jesus* as promulgated within the same Society of Jesus. In addition to the Saints of the Liturgical year, there are also included those feasts and solemnities (not holy days of obligation) whose celebrations occur on specific days in the Church calendar. Since Sundays, as well as those solemnities that always occur on Sunday, and holy days of obligation are liturgically celebrated with a greater participation on the part of the faithful, they are not included in this calendar.

The grade (solemnity, feast, memorial) of the celebration is given after the name of the day's saint or feast. When no grade is given for the celebration, it ranks as an optional memorial. When the memorials, etc. of the *General Liturgical Calendar of the Society of Jesus* differ from those of the *General Roman Calendar* and the *Proper Calendar for the Dioceses of the United States of America*, they are prefixed by a small cross (+).

January 2
Sts. Basil the Great and Gregory Nazianzen
Bishops and Doctors
Memorial

Sts. Basil and Gregory Nazianzen share a common feast, not only because they were contemporaries, but because they were also friends since the time they were fellow students. Basil was born in Pontus in Asia Minor, about 329, and studied in Caesarea, Constantinople, and Athens. Basil and Gregory were baptized together in 358 and Gregory subsequently joined Basil in living an ascetical life. Basil was ordained a priest about 365 and then in 370 was chosen Bishop of Caesarea. As bishop he championed the faith defined at Nicaea (325) and opposed the heretical Arian teaching that did away with the divinity of the Son and the Spirit. Through his preaching and writing he prepared the way for the Arians to return to orthodoxy. He died in Caesarea on January 1, 379.

St. Gregory Nazianzen was born in Arianzus, near Nazianzus, in Cappadocia, about 330. His father was Bishop of Nazianzus. Gregory first met Basil in Caesarea, and was later with him in Athens. Gregory was ordained a priest in 362, and then in 372 he was consecrated Bishop of Sasima, but remained in Nazianzus helping his aged father. In 379 Gregory was called to Constantinople to encourage the Nicene Catholics in their battle against the Arians. He became Bishop of Constantinople in 380 and participated in the Council of Constantinople (381), but when controversy arose about his being Bishop of Constantinople, he resigned his see and returned to Nazianzus, where he spent his time writing in defense of the Church's teaching. He died at Arianzus on January 25, about 390. Because of Basil's and Gregory's numerous and important writings, they are honored as Doctors of the Church.

January 4
St. Elizabeth Ann Seton, Religious
Memorial

St. Elizabeth Ann Seton is the foundress of the American Sisters of Charity, and the first born American to be canonized a saint. She was born Elizabeth Ann Bayley on August 28, 1774, in New York City; both her parents were Episcopalians and she was brought up in that faith. She married (January 25, 1794) William Magee Seton, a wealthy New York merchant, and the couple had five children. During a visit to Italy, Mr. Seton died (December 1803), and there Mrs. Seton, having become acquainted with an Italian Catholic family, began to learn about the Catholic faith. She returned to New York and was received into the Church (March 1805), but when her friends abandoned her because of her conversion, she accepted an invitation and went to Baltimore, where she opened (1808) a school for girls. After several young ladies joined in her educational work, they agreed to form a sisterhood. In the following year Elizabeth Ann went to Emmitsburg, Maryland, where she founded her congregation, the Sisters of Charity. As the number of sisters grew, so did the number of their schools and orphanages; Mother Seton's schools were the first in what eventually grew into the American parochial school system. She died at Emmitsburg on January 4, 1821, and was canonized by Pope Paul VI in 1975. The opening prayer of today's Mass summarizes St. Elizabeth Ann's life when it refers to her as "wife and mother, educator and foundress."

January 5
St. John Neumann, Bishop
Memorial

St. John Nepomucene Neumann is the first United States bishop to be canonized a saint. He was born in Prachatitz, Bohemia (modern Czechoslovakia), on March 28, 1811. While studying at the seminary in Prague, he decided to be a missionary in the United States; he finished his studies in 1835 and shortly afterwards left his homeland. When he arrived (June 2, 1836) in New York City, he was wearing the only clothes he owned and in his pockets he had but one dollar. He was accepted by Bishop Dubois of New York and was ordained a priest on June 25, 1836. He spent the next four years as a parish priest in Buffalo, working among German-speaking immigrants. He then entered the Redemptorist Order; his next pastoral assignments took him to Pittsburgh and Baltimore, also among German immigrants. Pope Pius IX appointed him fourth Bishop of Philadelphia and he was ordained on March 28, 1852. During his eight years as bishop he built eighty churches and organized Philadelphia's diocesan school system. At first he was not well received--he did speak with an accent and looked more like a laborer than a bishop--but in time the people came to know that they had a saint in their midst. He died of a heart attack on January 5, 1860, while walking along a Philadelphia street. He was canonized by Pope Paul VI in 1977.

January 6
Bl. André Bessette, Religious

The name of Bl. André is closely linked with that of St. Joseph. He was born Alfred Bessette on April 9, 1845, near the village of Saint-Grégoire d'Iberville, in the diocese of Montreal, Canada. By the time he was twelve he lost both parents, and since he had to go to work when still a young teenager, his formal education was necessarily limited. His jobs were varied, and there was a period when he worked (1863-1867) in a factory in New York. Upon his return to Canada he entered (November 1870) the Congregation of the Holy Cross as a brother, and received the name André. For most of his years in religious life he served as porter for the College of Notre Dame in Montreal. Br. André always had great devotion to St. Joseph, and he helped construct the first chapel dedicated to St. Joseph on the side of Mount Royal. The small chapel opened in 1904 and since Br. André spent much of his time there, he was made its custodian. The chapel soon became a place of pilgrimage, and as the number of pilgrims increased, so did miracles, all attributed to the prayers of the humble and holy Br. André. He cared for the shrine until his death in Montreal on January 6, 1937. He was beatified by Pope John Paul II in 1982. What was once a small chapel is now a basilica, where pilgrims from all parts of Canada and the United States come to honor St. Joseph and the humble devoted Br. André.

January 7
St. Raymond of Penyafort, Priest

St. Raymond was born at his family's Penyafort castle in Villafranca de Penadés, near Barcelona, Spain, about 1180. After completing his studies in Barcelona, he taught for a while, but then went to Bologna, Italy, to study canon law. He received his law degree in 1218, and then returned to Barcelona, where he became a canon at the cathedral. When he was in his forties he entered the Dominican Order, and since he was a renowned canonist Pope Gregory IX called him (1230) to Rome to collect and arrange the papal decrees in a single volume. This he did (*Decretals of Gregory IX*), and the collection eventually became the foundation for the Church's Canon Law. He returned (1236) to Barcelona and was elected (May 22, 1238) third Master General of the Dominicans. After he gave the Dominican Constitutions their final form, he resigned his office (June 2, 1240) and returned to Spain where he spent the remaining thirty-five years of his life working among the Moors and Jews. To help convert the Moors, he established (1245) a school of Arabic studies and asked St. Thomas Aquinas (see January 28) to write a text (*Summa contra gentiles*) that could be used in their conversion. He died in Barcelona on January 6, 1275, and was canonized by Pope Clement VIII in 1601. Since St. Raymond had written a very famous book to help confessors, the prayer of today's Mass mentions his "ministry to sinners."

January 13
St. Hilary, Bishop and Doctor

St. Hilary was born at Poitiers, France, about 315, and he became a Christian through his reading of the Bible. Hilary was chosen Bishop of Poitiers in 353, and his years as bishop were taken up in disputes with the Arians and in upholding the Church's teaching on Christ's divinity. While attending (356) a council of bishops at Béziers, in southern France, he refused to join the others in condemning St. Athanasius (see May 2) for his orthodox stand against the Arians. Hilary was, as a result, sent into exile to Phrygia in Asia Minor. During his four years in exile, he wrote two of his most important books, *On the Trinity*, which was directed against Arian teaching, and *On Synods*, which was a history of the eastern Church at that time. Hilary returned to his see in 361 and continued to undo the damage caused by the Arians in Gaul and northern Italy. He died in Poitiers on January 13, 367. He was the leading Latin theologian of his age, and Pope Pius IX declared him a Doctor of the Church in 1851. When the opening prayer in today's Mass says that "St. Hilary defended the divinity of Christ," this is a reference to his writing and his long struggle against the Arians.

January 17
St. Anthony, Abbot
Memorial

St. Anthony was born in Comus, Upper Egypt, about 250. As a young man he was given to prayer, and one day, hearing the Gospel read in church, he decided to give his possessions away and live as an ascetic. He found (269) a solitary place for himself near his village and there spent his time in prayer, penance, and manual labor. About 285, he left for the Egyptian desert, where he lived as a hermit. In due time stories began to spread about his holiness and disciplined life, his battles with the devil, and his miracles. The consequence was that other solitaries came to seek his advice and, eventually, they built their hermitages in the vicinity of Anthony's. Since Anthony now had disciples and had become their spiritual guide, he formed (305) them into a group and led them in the way of perfection and holiness. But Anthony was made for the solitary life of a hermit, and after about five years with his monks he returned (310) to the Egyptian desert, and there he died in 356, at age 105. His life was written by St. Athanasius (see May 2) in the year following Anthony's death, and in it Anthony is portrayed as the ideal monk and the "patriarch" of monks. The book (*Life of*

Anthony) had an immense influence in the early Christian world, and has always been valued as a spiritual classic. Ever since the fifth century St. Anthony's feast has been celebrated on January 17, as the date of his death. The opening prayer of today's Mass reminds us that St. Anthony renounced the world and sought solitude, and the prayer after Communion speaks of his conquering the powers of darkness.

+January 19
Bl. James Salès, Priest, and William Saultemouche, Religious; Melchior Grodecz and Stephen Pongrácz, Priests; Ignatius de Azevedo Priest, and Companions; James Bonnaud, Priest, and Companions, Martyrs

Today the Jesuit family commemorates the martyrdoms of sixty-seven of its brethren, all Blessed, who died for the Catholic faith between the years 1593 and 1792.

Fr. James Salès (b. 1556) and Br. William Saultemouche (b. 1557) were martyred in Aubenas, France, on February 7, 1593, and were beatified by Pope Pius XI in 1926.

Frs. Melchior Grodecz (b. 1584) and Stephen Pongrácz (b. 1583) were martyred at Kosice, in today's Czechoslovakia; Fr. Grodecz died on September 7, 1619, and Fr. Pongrácz on September 8. They were beatified by Pope Pius X in 1904.

Fr. Ignatius de Azevedo (b. 1527) and thirty-nine fellow Jesuits were martyred (July 15 and 16, 1570) off the Canary Islands, while on their way to the mission in Brazil. They were beatified by Pope Pius IX in 1854.

Fr. James Bonnaud (b. 1740) and twenty-two French Jesuits were martyred (September 2-5, 1792) in France during the years of the French Revolution. They were beatified by Pope Pius XI in 1926.

January 20
St. Fabian, Pope and Martyr

St. Fabian was a Roman and became pope on January 10, 236. Only a few things are actually known about him. It was he who divided Rome into seven ecclesiastical districts, with a deacon in charge of each, and it was he who brought the bodies of the martyrs Sts. Pontian and Hippolytus (see August 13), from Sardinia and gave them fitting burial in Rome. When the persecution of Decius (emperor 249-251) broke out in 250, Pope Fabian was arrested and was among the first to die (January 20, 250), most probably while in prison, and probably because of maltreatment. His body was placed in the papal crypt in the cemetery of Callistus and sometime later was transferred to the Basilica of St. Sebastian, where it was discovered in 1915.

Same day
St. Sebastian, Martyr

St. Sebastian may have been born in Milan, Italy. Not much is known of his life, but it is certain that he suffered in Rome during the persecution of Diocletian (emperor 284-305), sometime between the years 297 and 305. An account of Sebastian's martyrdom was written in 450, some 150 years after his death. According to this account, which is not completely reliable, he was an army officer, and since he was a Christian he was sentenced to death--to be shot by archers, who were his fellow soldiers. Through the generous ministrations of a widow named Irene, he recovered from his wounds and rather than fleeing Rome, he presented himself before the emperor, who then had him clubbed to death. Sebastian was buried in the catacombs on the Appian way, where the Basilica of St. Sebastian now stands.

Devotion to him spread very quickly among Romans and by the year 354 his feast was celebrated on January 20, as the date of his death.

January 21
St. Agnes, Virgin and Martyr
Memorial

St. Agnes was, at one time, one of the more popular saints in the Church, nevertheless, the only certain facts we have of her are that she was a Roman and that she was martyred and was buried on Rome's Via Nomentana, sometime during the second half of the third century or the beginning of the fourth. A church was built over her tomb in 349, and as early as 354, her feast was celebrated there on January 21, as the date of her death.

Tradition claims that when Agnes was about thirteen or fourteen she was being pressed into marriage, but since she chose to remain a virgin consecrated to God, she declined the marriage offers and admitted that she was a Christian. When she subsequently refused to offer incense to idols, the Roman governor sought a variety of ways to break her will. He first placed her in a brothel, but no one touched her. When ordered to be burned alive, the winds carried the flames away from Agnes and burned her would-be executioners. Finally, she was beheaded. The year of her martyrdom is sometimes given as 304 or 305. The opening prayer of today's Mass tells us that God can transform what the world considers as weakness into a strength that can put worldly power to shame, as Agnes' virginity withstood the threats of Rome's pagan governor.

January 22
St. Vincent, Deacon and Martyr

St. Vincent was born of a prominent family in Huesca, Spain, sometime in the second half of the third century. As a youth he studied under Valerius, Bishop of Saragossa, who also ordained him a deacon and placed him in charge of distributing alms to the poor and of caring for widows and orphans. At the outbreak (304) of the persecution of Diocletian (emperor 284-305), Dacian, the governor of Valencia (Spain), began the persecution in his region by arresting Valerius and Vincent. Both bishop and deacon were bound in chains and taken to Valencia, where Dacian interrogated them. Unable to get either to renounce his Christian faith, Dacian then exiled Valerius and ordered Vincent to be tortured. Torture could not persuade Vincent to deny his God, but it did allow him to pass from this earth to paradise (304). After Dacian had Vincent's body thrown into the sea, it was retrieved and appropriately buried. Of all those who suffered martyrdom in Spain during the first centuries of the Church, St. Vincent the Deacon was one of the most popular. Devotion to him spread widely and the *Hieronymian Martyrology* (about 450) records January 22 as the date of his death.

January 24
St. Francis de Sales, Bishop and Doctor
Memorial

St. Francis de Sales was born on August 21, 1567, near Annecy, in Savoy. Since his family was of the nobility, he was educated to be a gentleman. After early studies at Annecy, he went (1582) to Paris for his humanities, and then went (1588) to the University of Padua to study law in preparation for a government position. He received his law degree (1591), but a career in the world was not to his liking and in December 1593 he was ordained to the priesthood. The following year he went as a missionary to the Chablais, where he visited village after village trying to make converts. To help him in his task he wrote and distributed leaflets explaining the Catholic faith. After a few years his missionary work bore fruit, for many of the inhabitants became Catholics. On December 8, 1602, he was ordained Bishop of Geneva; he was an ideal bishop but he is better known for his writings. His sermons and conferences are numerous, and his most famous works are the *Introduction to a Devout Life* (1608) and the *Treatise on the Love of God* (1616). These books were popular when first written, and are still appreciated and read today. In 1610 he helped St. Jane Frances de Chantal (see August 18) found the Visitation Order. He died in Lyons on December 28, 1622, and was buried at Annecy on the following January 24, the date when his memorial is liturgically celebrated. He was canonized by Pope Alexander VII in 1665, and Pope Pius IX declared him a Doctor of the Church in 1877. Today's prayer speaks of St. Francis' "compassion to befriend all men on the way to salvation"; this was his motive in writing the two spiritual classics mentioned earlier.

January 25
Conversion of St. Paul, Apostle
Feast

Today we commemorate the day when our Lord, by the power of His grace, transformed a zealous persecutor into an impassioned apostle. Saul of Tarsus was brought up as a Pharisee and an enemy of Jesus Christ. After the death of St. Stephen (see December 26), at which he was present (Acts 7:58), Saul participated in a fierce persecution against the Christians. He "began to harass the church. He entered house after house, dragged men and women out, and threw them into jail" (Acts 8:3). He was then empowered to go to Damascus to arrest and bring to Jerusalem anyone who lived according to the new way (Acts 9:2). As Saul approached Damascus it was then that the Lord intervened. By means of a sudden flash of light Saul was thrown to the ground and converted. He who was once a determined persecutor now became a vessel of election. Today's Mass offers a choice of first readings (Acts 22:3-16 or Acts 9:1-22); both narrate the events of Paul's conversion. This feast originated in Gaul in the sixth century and is celebrated on January 25, the presumed date of the transfer of the relics of St. Paul to the Constantinian basilica on the Ostian Way.

January 26
Sts. Timothy and Titus, Bishops
Memorial

Sts. Timothy and Titus were St. Paul's faithful coworkers. Timothy was born in Lystra in Lycaonia, and when Paul visited that city (about 50), Timothy, a recent convert, was so highly recommended that Paul took him with him on his second missionary journey (Acts 16:1-4). Timothy was Paul's constant companion and undertook special missions for him, e.g., to the Thessalonians (1 Thess. 3:2) and to the Corinthians (1 Cor. 4:17). He was also imprisoned for a time, and then released (Heb. 13:23). In his letters Paul refers to Timothy as "my beloved and faithful son" (1 Cor. 4:17) and "my child whom I love" (2 Tim. 1:2). Paul appointed him Bishop of Ephesus (1 Tim. 1:3), and addressed two pastoral letters to him. Timothy is said to have been martyred in the year 97, under Nerva (emperor 96-98).

Titus, perhaps a native of Antioch, may have been a convert of Paul's, and is first mentioned in the New Testament when he accompanies Paul to Jerusalem (in the year 49 or 50), to attend a council (Gal. 2:1). In his letters Paul refers to Titus as his "traveling companion" (2 Cor. 8:16) and "my own true child in one common faith" (Tit. 1:4). Paul likewise placed him in charge of the collection in Corinth for the Jerusalem community (2 Cor. 8:6). With Paul he went to Crete and there he was left to organize the Church (Tit. 1:5); he is thus considered the first Bishop of Crete. Paul sent him to Dalmatia (2 Tim. 4:10) for a time; he then returned to Crete, where he died at an advanced age, perhaps in his late nineties. It is appropriate that the memorial of St. Paul's two closest collaborators, Sts. Timothy and Titus, be liturgically celebrated on the day following the commemoration of St. Paul's conversion. Today's Mass offers a choice of first readings; the first is taken from the beginning of Paul's second letter to Timothy (1:1-8), and the second is the opening verses of Paul's letter to Titus (1:1-5).

January 27
St. Angela Merici, Virgin

St. Angela Merici was born in Desenzano, Italy, probably on March 21, 1474. As a young lady she occupied herself in performing good works in her native town, but in 1506, when she was thirty-two years old, she had a vision in which she was told that she would "found a society of virgins at Brescia." Ten years later she was invited (1516) to Brescia to stay with Catherine Patengola, a widow, who had just lost two sons by death. Living in Brescia Angela noticed that the city's poor girls were without schooling and so she began catechetical work among them. In 1531 she organized a group of twelve girls to help her in her work, and then in 1535, when the group numbered twenty-eight, she formed them into the Company of St. Ursula. This was the first religious congregation founded for the education and training of young girls. Angela was convinced that the society of her time needed to be re-Christianized, and to accomplish this, she had to begin by educating girls, the wives and mothers of tomorrow. Angela died in Brescia on January 27, 1540, and was canonized by Pope Pius VII in 1807. The opening prayer today speaks of St. Angela's "charity and wisdom", a wisdom that saw the needs of her time and a charity that led her to respond to them.

January 28
St. Thomas Aquinas, Priest and Doctor
Memorial

St. Thomas Aquinas is the greatest theologian that the Church has ever had. He was born in Roccasecca, near Monte Cassino, Italy, about 1225, and was the son of Landolf of Aquino, Lord of Roccasecca. When Thomas was about six years of age (1231), his parents gave him to the Benedictine monastery in Monte Cassino as an oblate, that is, with a view of his eventually becoming a monk. There he studied until 1239 when he was sent to a Benedictine school in Naples. In April 1244, rather than entering the Benedictine Order, Thomas became a Dominican, and when his parents heard what their son had done, they physically carried him home. The following year, however, he was permitted to rejoin the Dominicans. He then studied in Paris (1245-1248) and Cologne (1248-1252), and returned (1252) to Paris for his doctorate. From 1256-1259 he was a professor in Paris; he subsequently returned to Italy and taught at Orvieto (1261-1265) and Rome (1265-1267). He again taught in Paris (1269-1272), but after three years he was once more in Naples. In 1274 Thomas was invited to attend the Council of Lyons (France), but not long after he had left Naples he fell ill and asked to be taken to the nearby Cistercian Abbey of Fossanova. There he died on March 7, 1274. He was canonized by Pope John XXII in 1323, and in 1567 Pope Pius V declared him a Doctor of the Church. St. Thomas' many writings in philosophy and theology have established him as the greatest thinker that the Church has produced. His *Summary of Sacred Theology* has been used as a text since the time it was first written. St. Thomas' memorial is celebrated on January 28, the date when his relics were transferred (1369) from Italy to the Dominican monastery in Toulouse, France.

January 31
St. John Bosco, Priest
Memorial

St. John Bosco was born at Castelnuovo d'Asti, near Turin, Italy, on August 16, 1815. Since his father had died when he was only two, the family knew poverty. With the encouragement of St. Joseph Cafasso, John entered (1835) the diocesan seminary and was ordained a priest in 1841. Soon after his ordination he gathered several young apprentices about him and taught them their catechism. He then opened a hospice for poor orphan boys, and in time added workshops, such as shoemaking, tailoring, and printing. Don Bosco, as he was known, encouraged the young men to learn a trade so that they could not only earn a living and raise families, but also be profitable members of society. In his own way Don Bosco was a forerunner in vocational training. When the number of boys under his care grew, Don Bosco trained (1850) teachers for the boys, and later (1854) these teachers placed themselves under the patronage of St. Francis de Sales (see January 24). In 1859 Don Bosco formed this group into a religious congregation, the Society of St. Francis de Sales, more commonly known as "Salesians." In 1872 he helped St. Maria Mazzarello found the Daughters of Mary, Help of Christians, who did similar work among girls. Don Bosco died on January 31, 1888, in Turin, and was canonized by Pope Pius XI in 1934. When today's opening prayer affirms that St. John Bosco was "a teacher and father to the young," this is a reference to his work among the young which is now continued by the two religious congregations he founded.

February 2
Presentation of the Lord
Feast

Our Lord's being presented in the Temple was the fulfillment of two Mosaic laws: that every first-born male was to be consecrated to the Lord (Ex. 13:2), and that the mother of the new-born son was to be purified in the Temple on the fortieth day after the birth (Lev. 12:2-8). Because both laws were fulfilled on the same day, this feast became known in Rome, in the eighth century, as the Purification of Our Lady, but in 1969 it was given its original title of the Presentation of the Lord. In the East this feast of the Presentation was also called *Hypapante* or "Encounter," because of the encounter of Jesus with the aged Simeon, which is likewise narrated in today's Gospel (Luke 2:22-40). The procession on this day dates back to the third century, and candles are blessed because of Simeon's prophecy that Christ will be "a revealing light to the Gentiles." The prayer at the blessing of the candles echoes that prophecy.

February 3
St. Blase, Bishop and Martyr

St. Blase was born in Sebaste, Armenia (today's Sivas, Turkey), became bishop of that city, and was martyred under Licinius (emperor 308-324) about the year 316. Not much more is known about him. Tradition has it that when persecution came to Sebaste, he was forced to hide in a cave, but was later discovered by animal hunters. He was subsequently tortured and beheaded at the orders of the pagan governor Agricolaus. By the sixth century he was invoked in the East for ailments of the throat; this is based on a story that while in prison he healed a young boy who was choking because of a fishbone lodged in his throat. Devotion to St. Blase took root in the West about the ninth century, and by the late Middle Ages he was one of the more popular saints. The blessing of throats with candles began in the sixteenth century, when devotion to St. Blase was at its highest.

Same day
St. Ansgar, Bishop

Since St. Ansgar had been the first missionary to Denmark and Sweden, he is known as the "Apostle of the North." Ansgar was born near Corbie, in northern France, about the year 801. He was educated by the Benedictines at Corbie and then entered (about 814) the Benedictine Order. He was later assigned (822) to the new monastery at Corvey (Westphalia, Germany), and about 826, after King Harold of Denmark had been converted to Christianity at the Frankish court of Louis the Pious, Ansgar traveled with him to Denmark as a missionary. Since he met with little success in Denmark, he left (829) and accepted the invitation to do missionary work in Sweden. After a year and a half in Sweden, he was recalled and appointed (832) Bishop of Hamburg, Germany. Ansgar worked in Hamburg for thirteen years, until the Northmen invaded (845) the land, burned the city and razed it to the ground. In 847 he became Bishop of Bremen and once more sent missionaries to the northern countries. He himself again went to Denmark and converted Eric, King of Jutland; he returned to Sweden (852-853), and there King Olaf became a Christian. Ansgar returned to Bremen and died there on February 3, 865. Since he was revered as a saint by the faithful in Germany, Pope Nicholas I (858-867) confirmed his cult. Today's prayer reminds us that through St. Ansgar's missionary efforts he brought "the light of Christ to many nations."

+February 4
St. John de Brito, Priest; Bl. Rudolph Acquaviva, Priest, and Companions; Francis Pacheco, Charles Spinola, Priests, and Companions; James Berthieu, Priest; Leo Mangin, Priest, and Companions, Martyrs
Memorial

One Jesuit saint and forty-four Jesuit blessed are liturgically commemorated today. All are martyrs and all died in what were missionary lands: India, Japan, Madagascar, and China.

St. John de Brito was born (March 1, 1647) in Lisbon, Portugal, and died in the Madura Mission, India, on February 4, 1693. He was canonized by Pope Pius XII in 1947.

Bl. Rudolph Acquaviva (b. October 2, 1550) and his four companions also died in India, but on the Salsette peninsula. They met their martyrdom on July 25, 1583, and were beatified by Pope Leo XIII in 1893.

Bl. Francis Pacheco (d. June 20, 1626), Charles Spinola (d. September 10, 1622), and thirty-two Jesuit companions died for the faith between the years 1617 and 1632, while doing missionary work in Japan. They were beatified by Pope Pius IX in 1867.

Bl. James Berthieu was a Frenchman (b. November 28, 1838), who went as a missionary to Madagascar and was martyred there on June 8, 1896. He was beatified by Pope Paul VI in 1965.

Bl. Leon Mangin (b. July 30, 1857) and three Jesuit companions, all Frenchmen, were missionaries in China and gave their lives (July 19-20, 1900) for the faith during the Boxer Rebellion. They were beatified by Pope Pius XII in 1955.

Today's opening prayer speaks of these martyrs as missionaries "who [were] fearless in proclaiming the word of our Lord."

February 5
St. Agatha, Virgin and Martyr
Memorial

St. Agatha was probably born in Catania, Sicily, during the first half of the third century, and was martyred in Catania during the persecution of Decius (emperor 249-251), about the year 251. As in the case of other early martyrs, details of St. Agatha's life are lacking and only legends remain. Accordingly, she was sent to a brothel so that she would be forced to deny her faith. Because she remained steadfast in her resolves, her breasts were cut off, but she was subsequently healed when St. Peter appeared to her in prison. A few days later she underwent further tortures, and as a result of these, she died. The early martyrologies agree in assigning February 5 as the date of her death. Devotion to St. Agatha spread very quickly through Sicily and into Italy, and Pope Symmachus (498-514) erected a church in her honor on Rome's Via Aurelia. Her popularity is evidenced by the fact that her name had been added to the Roman Canon. The opening prayer of today's Mass states that Agatha found favor with God because of her chastity and her courage in professing the faith.

February 6
Sts. Paul Miki, Religious, and Companions, Martyrs
Memorial

Three Jesuits (two scholastics and a coadjutor brother) were martyred at Nagasaki, Japan, on February 5, 1597, together with twenty-three other religious and lay-people. Paul Miki was born in Japan in 1564 and became a Jesuit in 1586. Because of the persecution then raging in Japan, he and his companions were arrested and sentenced to death by crucifixion. Crowded into carriages, they were taken on the long and difficult ride to Nagasaki. When they arrived at the hill of execution, now known as the Hill of Martyrs, and saw crosses awaiting them, their hearts burst into song. They rushed to the crosses and waited for the executioners to fasten the ropes. From his cross Paul preached his final sermon: he invited the onlookers to accept Christianity, said that he was joyfully giving his life for Christ, and then forgave his executioners. At a prearranged signal, the soldiers standing by each cross thrust lances into each martyr's breast. The two other Jesuits to die with Paul Miki were the scholastic John

Soan de Goto (b. 1578), and the coadjutor brother James Kisai (b. 1533). All twenty-six martyrs were canonized by Pope Pius IX in 1862. The prayer in today's Mass refers to the manner in which these martyrs entered into the joy of eternal life.

February 8
St. Jerome Emiliani, Priest

St. Jerome Emiliani spent his entire priestly life in caring for orphans and abandoned children, and so it is not surprising that Pope Pius XI declared him their patron in 1928. St. Jerome was born in Venice, Italy, in 1486. His father was of senatorial rank, and he himself was educated and trained to follow in his father's footsteps. In early 1511 he enlisted in the Venetian army, but was captured the following August. While in prison he underwent a conversion and promised to dedicate himself to the Lord if released. He, in fact, was freed on September 27 of that year--he merely walked out of prison without anyone taking any notice of him. He returned to his family and thought of how he could better serve God. He became a priest in 1518. In 1527, when a plague broke out in Venice, he worked in the hospitals for the incurables. Then, because of the number of orphans roaming the city streets, he established (1528) a home for them, taught them catechism and gave them vocational training. His orphanage proved successful and he extended his work to other cities as well. In 1532 he and his two priest fellow-workers formed the Society of the Servants of the Poor and devoted their time and efforts to caring for orphans and abandoned children. St. Jerome died in the town of Somasca, near Bergamo, Italy, on February 8, 1537, caring for victims of the plague. Some thirty years later (1568), his society became a religious Order with the name Clerks Regular Somaschi. He was canonized by Pope Clement XIII in 1767. The prayer of the Mass today recalls that St. Jerome was "a father and a friend of orphans."

February 10
St. Scholastica, Virgin
Memorial

St. Scholastica was the sister, perhaps the twin sister, of St. Benedict (see July 11), the founder of monasticism in the West. She was born in Nursia, Italy, about 480. At first she lived a contemplative form of life at home, but when companions asked to join her, she founded a monastery at Plombariola, a few miles south of Monte Cassino. Since her brother had already established his monastery there, he now undertook the spiritual direction of Scholastica's group. St. Gregory the Great (see September 3) writes in his *Dialogues* that Benedict and Scholastica used to meet once a year to pray and to have a chat together. He also relates that when Scholastica died, about 547, Benedict saw a dove ascend into heaven and, thus, he knew that his sister had departed this world. St. Scholastica is acknowledged as the foundress of the women's branch of the Benedictine Order, and from as early as the eighth century her memorial has been celebrated at Monte Cassino on February 10.

February 11
Our Lady of Lourdes

It was on February 11, 1858, that Bernadette Soubirous and two other young girls left their small village, in the parish of Lourdes in southeastern France, to gather kindling wood for the fires at home.

When Bernadette was alone on the shores of the river, near the grotto of Massabielle, our Lady unexpectedly appeared to her. The apparitions continued through February and into April, but Bernadette was never certain who "the beautiful Lady in white" really was. On March 25, the feast of the Annunciation, Bernadette asked her: "Would you please tell me who you are?" The answer she heard was: "I am the Immaculate Conception." From the time of our Lady's apparitions in that grotto, Lourdes has become the most famous Marian shrine in Western Europe. Countless are the pilgrims who go there each year, and frequent are the miracles performed--physical healing as well as spiritual. In 1890 Pope Leo XIII permitted the local diocese, where Lourdes is located, to celebrate this feast; then Pope Pius X extended (1907) it to the universal church. When today's prayer refers to Mary as "the sinless mother of God", it is but reiterating the name that our Lady gave herself when she said "I am the Immaculate Conception."

February 14
Sts. Cyril, Monk, and Methodius, Bishop
Memorial

Sts. Cyril and Methodius were blood brothers and were born in Thessalonica (modern day Salonika) Greece. Cyril, whose true name was Constantine, was born about 826, and Methodius, whose name was Michael, was born about 815. They received the names Cyril and Methodius when they became monks. Though both brothers spoke Greek they also knew the Slavonic language since many Macedonian Slavs lived in their area. After studies at Constantinople, Methodius accepted a government position in a Slavonic-speaking area, while Cyril taught philosophy. Methodius then

Cyril joined him. In 862, when Ratislav, Duke of Greater Moravia, requested missionaries capable of instructing the Slavs in their own language, Cyril, who had been ordained a priest, and Methodius were chosen for the task. In preparation for their mission, Cyril invented an alphabet (Glagolithic script), and translated the Gospels and the liturgical books into what is now known as Old Church Slavonic. Since the brothers used Slavonic and not Latin in the liturgy they ran into difficulty with the Bavarian priests in that same area, but when they went to Rome (867/868) Pope Hadrian II approved their use of the Slavonic liturgy. Cyril died in Rome on February 14, 869. Methodius was then consecrated Archbishop of Sirmium (today's Sremska Mitrovica in Yugoslavia) and returned to Moravia to continue his missionary work. He died at Velehrad (Czechoslovakia) on April 6, 885. Sts. Cyril and Methodius are honored as the "Apostles of the Slavs" and as patrons of Europe. They are also acknowledged as the fathers of Slavonic literature because of their invention of the alphabet and their translation of the Bible.

+February 15
Bl. Claude La Colombière, Priest

Bl. Claude La Colombière was born in Saint-Symphorien d'Ozon in southern France, on February 2, 1641. He entered the Society of Jesus in 1658, and after ordination was assigned (1675) to the Jesuit residence in Paray-le-Monial. In the Visitation convent of Paray, but unknown to Fr. Claude, our Lord was revealing the treasures of His Sacred Heart to Sister Margaret Mary Alacoque (see October 16) and Our Lord had told her "I will send you my faithful servant and perfect friend." Shortly after his arrival in Paray, Fr. Claude visited the convent and on that occasion Sr. Margaret Mary heard an interior voice say: "This is he whom I have sent to you." She told him of her revelations and from that time onward, both he and she worked to have the feast of the Sacred Heart established in the Church. After eighteen months in Paray, he was assigned (1676) to be preacher to the Duchess of York in London. England still had laws against Catholic priests, and in November 1678, Fr. Claude was unjustly accused and arrested for traitorous speech. While imprisoned in a damp dungeon, his health deteriorated so rapidly that he was released (January 1679) and sent back to France. He never regained his health, and in August 1681 he returned to Paray-le-Monial, where he died on February 15, 1682. He was beatified by Pope Pius XI in 1929. The prayer of today's Mass speaks of Bl. Claude as being our Lord's "faithful servant" and a "witness to the riches of [His] love."

February 17
Seven Founders of the Order of Servites

In thirteenth-century Florence, seven laymen, all prominent merchants and members of a confraternity known as the Brothers of Penance, decided (1233) to abandon their homes, their careers, and their wealth and retire to a place outside the city where they could live a life of prayer, poverty, and penance. The leader of the group was Bonfilius Monaldo (the others were Bartholomew Amidei, Benedict dell'Antella, John Bonagiunta, Alexis Falconieri, Gerard Sostegni, and Ricovero Uguccione). They chose the unfrequented slopes of Mount Senario as their place of habitation, and there they built a small chapel and hermitages for themselves. Several years later they returned to Florence and at the bishop's suggestion they formed themselves into a religious order and called themselves the Servants of Mary, or Servites. The first superior was Bonfilius (d. 1261) and under him the Order grew in numbers and spread to various Italian cities. The last of the seven founders to die was Alexis Falconieri, who always remained a coadjutor brother. He died on February 17, 1310, at 110 years of age. The seven founders were canonized by Pope Leo XIII in 1888. Their memorial is celebrated today, the anniversary of the death of St. Alexis Falconieri. Today's prayer recalls their coming together and forming a religious congregation under the patronage of our Lady, and thereby leading other souls to heaven.

February 21
St. Peter Damian, Bishop and Doctor

St. Peter Damian was born in Ravenna, Italy, in 1007. He taught school for a time in his native city, then was ordained a priest, and when he was about twenty-eight years of age he entered (1035) the Benedictine monastery at Fonte Avellana. He became prior of the monastery in 1043 and was known for his austere penitential practices and his revitalizing of the monastic spirit in his monks. During this period he wrote ascetical treatises for his monks, and he also wrote several treatises advocating reformation within the Church and among the clergy. As a result Pope Stephen IX made (1057) him Cardinal Bishop of Ostia. Peter Damian worked very closely with Pope Stephen and two successive popes and served them on several special diplomatic missions to France and Germany. He revisited Ravenna in 1072 to effect a reconciliation between that city and the pope, and on his return trip to Rome, he died at a Benedictine monastery in Faenza on the night of February 22-23, 1072. Peter Damian was immediately venerated by his monks as a saint. In 1828 Pope Leo XII approved his cult, extended its celebration to the universal Church, and declared him a Doctor of the Church.

February 22
Chair of St. Peter, Apostle
Feast

Today we commemorate Christ's granting of the primacy in the Church to the apostle Peter, and the Gospel (Matt. 16:13-19) of today's Mass relates how Christ gave Simon the name Peter, telling him: "you are 'Rock' and on this rock I will build my Church" (Matt. 16:18). The office or task that Peter was given was that of universal teacher and pastor of the faithful, and the symbol of that office is the cathedra, or chair and, hence, today's feast is called "Chair of St. Peter." Therefore, on this day we acknowledge Peter's pontifical authority as well as the pontifical authority invested in Peter's successor, our present pope. The prayers of the Mass speak of a unity in faith and love, a unity which is symbolized in Peter, on whom Christ chose to build His Church. A unity in faith and love with the pope today is a unity in faith and love with Peter, and ultimately with Christ our Lord.

February 23
St. Polycarp, Bishop and Martyr
Memorial

Only few details are known about the life of St. Polycarp. He was born about the year 69, was a disciple of St. John the Apostle, and was Bishop of Smyrna (modern Izmir, Turkey). He paid a visit to Rome (about 155), representing the churches of Asia Minor, to discuss with Pope Anicetus the date when the feast of Easter should be celebrated. The result of their meeting was that the Churches of the East and West were to continue to follow their respective systems of computing the date for Easter. Shortly after his return to Smyrna, he was arrested during a public festival, and when urged to betray his faith, he answered that he had followed Christ for eighty-six years and that he was not about to reject his King and Savior. He was consequently sentenced to be burned to death in the Stadium in Smyrna. Since the flames did not harm him, he was killed by the sword on February 23, 155/156.

March 3
Bl. Katharine Drexel, Virgin

Bl. Katharine Drexel was born into a prosperous and wealthy banking family in Philadelphia, on November 26, 1858. Her education was with private tutors and governesses. Upon the death of her parents, Katharine and her two sisters inherited a sizable fortune, but the Drexel sisters were not ones to squander money; they used it philanthropically. Katharine first became interested in the plight of Native Americans when members of the Bureau of Catholic Indian Missions approached her for help. She responded by building schools, churches, and convents. What the Indian missions needed, according to her friend Bishop O'Connor of Omaha, were priests, so during a visit (1886) with Pope Leo XIII she pleaded for priests for the Indians. But the pope responded: "Why not, my child, yourself become a missionary." Thereafter Katharine decided to enter religion, but unable to find a congregation that worked specifically with Indians and Blacks, she decided on founding her own. After two years of novitiate training with the Sisters of Mercy in Pittsburgh, she and a few companions founded (1891) the Sisters of the Blessed Sacrament for Indians and Colored People. Throughout her life she continued to disburse the income from her inheritance in building and maintaining schools among Indians in the Northwest and among Blacks in the South. The schools once built, were staffed by her own congregation. In 1915 she established Xavier University in New Orleans, a university for Blacks. Annually she traveled the country to inspect her foundations. It was on one such tour that she suffered (1935) a severe heart attack and, as a result, she had to curtail her travel and work. She then retired to the motherhouse, and spent her time in prayer. She died at Cornwells Heights, on March 3, 1955, at age ninety-seven. Though a millionaire, she chose to live in poverty so that she could help others in need. Bl. Katharine Drexel was beatified by Pope John Paul II in 1988.

March 4
St. Casimir

St. Casimir was born in Cracow, Poland, on October 3, 1458, the second son of Casimir IV, King of Poland and Grand Duke of Lithuania, and of Elizabeth of Austria. As a youth Casimir joined his father in his travels and campaigns, and when the king went to Lithuania for reasons of state (1481-1483), Casimir ruled as regent in Poland. He was especially known for his piety, devotion to the Blessed Sacrament and to the Blessed Virgin, and his generosity toward the poor. When marriage was suggested he rejected the idea since he would not renounce his self-imposed chastity. During an official visit to Lithuania he fell ill, died of consumption at the royal castle in Grodno on March 4,

1484, and was buried in the cathedral in Vilnius. He was only twenty-five years old. Casimir was canonized in 1521 by Pope Leo X, and is the patron saint of Poland and Lithuania. The prayer of today's Mass reminds us that to serve God is to reign; St. Casimir preferred to serve his eternal King rather than that he himself should be a temporal king.

March 7
Sts. Perpetua and Felicity, Martyrs
Memorial

St. Perpetua was a twenty-two-year-old noble lady living in Carthage (in modern Tunisia), and St. Felicity was her slave. Both were catechumens, and because they refused, during the persecution of Septimius Severus (emperor 193-211), to pay divine worship to the emperor, they were condemned to be thrown to the wild beasts. While in prison, they were baptized, and when it came time for them to be led to the amphitheater and to death, Perpetua and Felicity walked with so graceful a bearing that it seemed that they were entering heaven. After the beasts had attacked them, but did not kill them, they were beheaded by a gladiator. Their martyrdom took place on March 7, 202 or 203. A basilica was built over their tombs in ancient Carthage and both their names were added to the Roman Canon.

March 8
St. John of God, Religious

St. John Ciudad was born in Montemor-o-Novo, Portugal, on March 8, 1495. He was taken to Spain as a child and there he became a shepherd in Castile. When he was twenty-seven years old he joined the

Count of Oropesa's forces in fighting the French and he later fought against the Turks in Vienna. When forty, he gave up the military life and returned to Spain. Saddened and disturbed about his former dissolute life, John entered upon a life of penance. In Granada he opened a small religious goods store and cared for the sick poor. He eventually rented a house to take care of the abandoned sick, and later on he founded a hospital in Granada for them. Other individuals joined him, and because of his heroic charity the people began calling him "John of God." His little group of helpers expanded and eventually they formed the religious congregation of Brothers Hospitallers, which still cares for those sick in body and in spirit. After years of tireless service, John fell ill and died on March 8, 1550, his fifty-fifth birthday. He was canonized by Pope Alexander VIII in 1690. Pope Leo XIII proclaimed (1886) him and St. Camillus de Lellis (see July 14) patrons of hospitals and the sick, and in 1930 Pope Pius XI declared St. John of God the heavenly patron of nurses. The opening prayer of today's Mass recalls his love and compassion for others.

March 9
St. Frances of Rome, Religious

St. Frances was born in Rome in 1384, a member of the noble Busso family. Obedient to her parents' wishes, she was married at a very early age to Lorenzo dei Ponziani, a wealthy landowner in Rome's Trastevere section. During her years of married life, she bore three children and was an exemplary mother and wife. Those were also difficult years for Rome, when war, famine, and plague ravaged the city. With her husband's consent Frances devoted herself to works of mercy: helping the poor, caring for the sick in their homes, and visiting hospitals. In 1425 she and several other ladies united to form a group of oblates, dedicated to works of charity. In 1433 these ladies began to live in community in the building known as Tor de' Specchi in the center of Rome, but Frances continued to live with her husband. Her reputation for charity became widespread and the people simply referred to her as "Frances of Rome." After the death of her husband (1435), she too went (March 21, 1436) to live in the community she had founded. She died in Rome on March 9, 1440, and was canonized by Pope Paul V in 1608. Her group, the Oblates of Tor de' Specchi, still exists today. The prayer in today's Mass speaks of Frances as "a unique example of love in marriage as well as in religious life."

March 17
St. Patrick, Bishop

St. Patrick, the apostle and patron of Ireland, was born in Roman Britain (Scotland?) about 389. When he was sixteen (405) he was seized by Irish raiders, taken to Ireland and sold as a slave. After six years of shepherding he escaped and returned to his homeland. The thought of some day returning to Ireland to convert the pagans living there impelled him to go to Gaul (modern France) to study for the priesthood. About 432 Pope Celestine I (422-432) had Patrick consecrated bishop and sent him to Ireland to succeed Bishop Palladius. Patrick travelled throughout the island and tirelessly preached the Gospel to eager ears. He made countless converts, established the Catholic Church, recruited clergy from Gaul and Britain, and founded many monastic communities. He is also said to have established (about 444) the primatial see of Ireland at Armagh. After nearly thirty years of fruitful evangelizing, he died about 461. Since the seventh century March 17 has been given as the date of St. Patrick's death.

March 18
St. Cyril of Jerusalem, Bishop and Doctor

St. Cyril was born of Christian parents about the year 313, in or near Jerusalem. He was ordained a priest about 345 and was placed in charge of preparing catechumens for baptism. The twenty-four instructions that he gave them in the church of the Holy Sepulchre in Jerusalem during Lent of 348 or 349, are still extant (*Catecheses*) and form a thorough introduction to the Catholic faith. Cyril became Bishop of Jerusalem about 350 at a time when the East was still troubled by the Arian heresy which erroneously held that Christ is a mere creature and not the son of God. Because he had maintained and preached that Christ is indeed the true son of God and is of the same nature as the Father, he was banished from his see by the Arians on three different occasions. He later played an important role at the second ecumenical council held in Constantinople in 381. He died in Jerusalem on March 18, 386, having been bishop for some thirty-five years, sixteen of which were spent in exile. Because of his writings explaining the faith, Pope Leo XIII declared (1882) him a Doctor of the Church.

March 19
St. Joseph, Husband of Mary
Solemnity

The only facts that we know of St. Joseph's life are those that we have in the Gospels: he was a carpenter, the husband of Mary, the foster-father of our Lord, and protector of the Holy Family. As early as the ninth century, German martyrologies have given the date of St. Joseph's death as March 19, but none give the reason why this date had been chosen. By the fourteenth century, the Franciscan and Servite Orders liturgically celebrated a feast honoring St. Joseph, but devotion to him did not become really widespread until after the preaching of St. Bernardine of Siena (see May 20) and the writings of St. Teresa of Jesus (see October 15). In 1476, the Franciscan pope, Sixtus IV, introduced St. Joseph's feast in Rome, and by 1621 it was inserted into the Church's universal calendar. In 1870 Pope Pius IX proclaimed Joseph the patron of the universal Church, and in 1962 Pope John XXIII added his name to the Roman Canon.

March 23
St. Turibius of Mogrovejo, Bishop

St. Turibius of Mogrovejo was born in Mayorga, near Valladolid, Spain, in November 1538. He studied and then taught law at Salamanca until 1574, when he was named inquisitor of Granada. In 1580 Pope Gregory XIII named him Archbishop of Lima, but since he was not yet ordained a priest, he at first humbly declined but then obeyed the pope's wishes. He was ordained a bishop in Seville in August 1580 and in September he sailed for the New World. In Peru Archbishop Turibius was a tireless missionary. During his twenty-five years there, he visited his vast diocese three times, held thirteen diocesan and three provincial synods. He saw to the reform of the clergy and ordered that catechisms be published in the language of the native Indians. He established the first seminary in the New World and encouraged the Indians to study for the priesthood. That the Catholic Church was firmly established in Peru is due to his missionary zeal. He fell ill while visiting his diocese and died at Saña on March 23, 1606. He was canonized by Pope Benedict XIII in 1726.

March 25
Annunciation of the Lord
Solemnity

Today we liturgically celebrate the Incarnation of God's Son, when the Word entered our human sphere and took unto Himself a human nature, joining His divine nature to our human mortality. He was conceived, through the power of the Holy Spirit, in the virginal womb of Mary of Nazareth, and from that moment on God was living among us. He became like us in all things, but sin. Nine months from this date we celebrate His birth in Bethlehem. In the early Church it was commonly believed that Christ was not only conceived on March 25, but that he likewise died on that date. This St. Augustine (354-430) states in his book *On the Trinity* (iv, 5) when he says: "The VIII Kalends of April [March 25] is both the day of His conception and His passion." This feast of the Annunciation of the Lord was most probably first liturgically celebrated in the church of Constantinople during the first half of the fifth century, but by the seventh century it was also widespread in the West.

April 2
St. Francis of Paola, Hermit

St. Francis was born in Paola, in Calabria, in southern Italy, on March 27, 1416. At age twelve he was placed in a Franciscan friary, in fulfillment of a promise that his parents had made to St. Francis of Assisi. After a year at the friary, he and his parents made pilgrimages to Rome, Assisi, Loreto, etc. Returning to Calabria, Francis, who was now going on fourteen, left home and became a hermit. Other young men in time joined him and they formed a group known as the Hermits of Saint Francis. Francis' reputation for holiness and for being a miracle worker spread through Italy and even into France, and when King Louis XI was dying he asked Francis to come and cure him. The holy hermit was disinclined to make the long trip, but when Pope Sixtus IV urged (1483) him to go, he obeyed. Rather than restoring the king to health, Francis, however, prepared him for death. Francis then remained in France and in 1492 he changed the name of his group to the Order of Minims to emphasize that they were "the least" in God's family. He died on Good Friday, April 2, 1507, at age ninety-one, near Tours, France, and was canonized by Pope Leo X in 1519.

April 4
St. Isidore, Bishop and Doctor

St. Isidore was most probably born in Seville, Spain, sometime between the years 560 and 570. He attended the monastic school where his older brother Leander was a monk, and later he himself entered the same monastery. When Leander died (about 600), Isidore succeeded him as Archbishop of Seville. During his years as archbishop, Isidore strengthened the Catholic Church in Spain by calling numerous provincial and national synods; he also presided over the famous Fourth Council of Toledo (633), which established liturgical uniformity throughout Spain and decreed a cathedral school in every diocese. He wrote many biblical, theological, and historical works (all of which have survived) and was considered the most learned man of his time. During the Middle Ages he was looked upon as "the Master," especially because of his *Etymologies*, a total of twenty books that formed a general encyclopedia and summary of all religious and secular learning up to his time. St. Isidore died in Seville on April 4, 636, and was canonized by Pope Clement VIII in 1598. In 1722 Pope Innocent XIII declared him a Doctor of the Church.

April 5
St. Vincent Ferrer, Priest

St. Vincent Ferrer was born in Valencia, Spain, January 23, 1350, and entered the Dominican Order when he was seventeen. Vincent's active years as a Dominican were the years of the Great Schism (1378-1417), when there were three popes, each claiming the allegiance of Catholics. So confusing and complicated was the period that the Catholics of the world had no way of knowing who was the true pope. Vincent opted for Pope Clement VII, then living in Avignon, France. When the Spanish Cardinal Pedro de Luna was elected (1394) Benedict XIII to succeed Clement VII, Vincent became his chaplain in Avignon, but when he realized that Benedict had no desire to heal the wound in the Church, he left Avignon knowing that Benedict could not then be the true pope. In 1399 he began his apostolate of preaching and spent twenty years traveling though Spain, northern Italy, Switzerland, France, and the Low Countries preaching the need of repentance and the coming of the judgment. So forceful were his sermons, which sometimes lasted three hours, that he became known as the "Angel of the Judgment." Vincent lived to see the end of the Great Schism in 1417, but he died two years later at Vannes, in Brittany, France, on

April 5, 1419. He was canonized by Pope Callistus III in 1455. The prayer in today's Mass recalls St. Vincent's preaching "the gospel of the last judgment."

April 7
St. John Baptist de la Salle, Priest
Memorial

St. John Baptist de la Salle was the founder of the Institute of the Brothers of the Christian Schools. He was born in Rheims, France, on April 30, 1651, and during his early years as a priest he soon perceived the need for free schools for poor boys, in which they would be given a basic education and would also be taught religion and trained to be good Christians. He opened his first school in Rheims and he likewise trained the teachers for the school. In 1684 he and his twelve teachers formed a religious congregation and called themselves Brothers of the Christian Schools. John Baptist was an innovator in the area of pedagogy: he replaced individual instruction with class instruction, stressed the need for a thorough knowledge of the vernacular, made religious instruction the center of the school day, and established the first normal school for the training of teachers. He died at Rouen on April 7, 1719, and was canonized by Pope Leo XIII in 1900. Pope Pius XII named him (1950) patron of teachers. Today's prayer in the Mass recalls his dedication in offering a Christian education to the young.

April 11
St. Stanislaus, Bishop and Martyr
Memorial

St. Stanislaus is the patron of Poland and was born at Szczepanów, in the diocese of Cracow, about 1030. After his ordination to the priesthood he became a canon at Cracow, and then in 1072 Pope Alexander II named him bishop of the city. At first he was on friendly terms with King Boleslaus II, but because of the king's injustices, cruelties, and dissolute manner of life, Stanislaus excommunicated him. Boleslaus viewed this action as treasonable, and on April 11, 1079, while Stanislaus was celebrating Mass in the church of St. Michael in Cracow, the king entered the church and murdered the bishop. Stanislaus was immediately regarded as a martyr and nine years after his death, his body was taken (1088) to the cathedral in Cracow where his tomb became a center of pilgrimage. He was canonized by Pope Innocent IV in 1253.

April 13
St. Martin I, Pope and Martyr

St. Martin was born in Todi, Italy, on an unrecorded date, and was a deacon in Rome when he became pope on July 5, 649. In October of that year he held a synod in Rome in which he affirmed the Catholic teaching that there are two wills in Christ, divine and human, and condemned the heretical teaching taught in the East that there was but one will coming from a single nature. The synod at the same time rejected the injunction of Constans II (emperor 641-688) to end all discusssion about Christ's wills. In view of Pope Martin's refusal to obey the imperial injunction, Constans had him arrested (January 17, 653) and taken to Constantinople. There the pope was brutally maltreated, publicly humiliated, and stripped of his episcopal robes. He was then flogged and condemned to exile. The pope left Constantinople in March 654 and was taken to Kherson in the Crimea, near Sevastopol, where after many hardships (famine, cold, and abusive treatment) he died on September 16, 655. He was immediately honored as a martyr. St. Martin's memorial, however, is celebrated on April 13, the date that it has always been celebrated in the East. The prayer of today's Mass speaks of the hardship, pain, and threats of death that never weakened St. Martin's faith and trust in God.

April 21
St. Anselm, Bishop and Doctor

St. Anselm was born in Aosta in northern Italy, about 1033; he studied in France and became a Benedictine monk at the abbey of Bec in Normandy in 1060. He was chosen abbot in 1078, and under his supervision the monastic school at Bec became a renowned center of learning. In 1093 he was named Archbishop of Canterbury, but because of conflicts with William II (Rufus), King of England, over the spiritual rights of the Church, Anselm went (1097) to Italy for support. With the death of William (1100), Anselm returned to Canterbury, but the same problems occurred with Henry I, and thus Anselm again went (1103) into exile. When Henry finally agreed to respect the Church's independence in appointing bishops, Anselm also agreed to return (1107). He died on April 21, 1109, and his cult was approved by Pope Alexander VI (1492-1503); in 1720 Pope Clement XI declared him a Doctor of the Church. St. Anselm was the foremost theologian of his age and often spoke about "faith seeking understanding" to emphasize the harmony between faith and human reason. The prayer in today's Mass adopts St. Anselm's expression when it asks that God's "gift of faith come to the aid of our understanding."

+April 22
The Blessed Virgin Mary
Mother of the Society of Jesus
Feast

Today the Society of Jesus celebrates our Lady's motherly care over the Society. At all important junctures in the life of St. Ignatius of Loyola (see July 31), our Lady had an important role to play, but April 22 is special to Jesuits because it was on that date in 1541 that Ignatius and companions pronounced their first Jesuit vows. Early on the morning of April 22, Friday of Easter week, Ignatius and companions made a pilgrimage to the seven churches of Rome and when they finally arrived at St. Paul Outside-the-Walls, Ignatius, as the newly elected general, celebrated Mass at our Lady's altar. Immediately before receiving Holy Communion, they all pronounced their vows in the newly formed Society of Jesus. Ignatius chose our Lady's altar as the place most suitable for the first Jesuits to pronounce their first vows; he knew that he and his companions, and those who were to follow them, would need our Lady's continued maternal protection. The opening prayer of today's Mass alludes to this event when it says that the Society of Jesus consecrated itself to God's glory in the presence of Mary.

April 23
St. George, Martyr

Very little is actually known about St. George. Tradition claims that he was a native of Cappadocia and a soldier, who was martyred (about 303) at Lydda (Lod in modern Israel), during the time of Diocletian (emperor 284-305). By the sixth century his cult was immensely popular and his tomb in Lydda a favorite place of pilgrimage. Because the faithful commonly referred to him as "the Great Martyr," legends soon began to set in, for example, his slaying of the dragon. When the crusaders of the eleventh century returned home, they brought with them devotion to St. George, whom they had adopted as their patron since he was usually depicted as a knight or a soldier. Devotion to the martyr also became widespread in the West; in 1222 a synod held at Oxford, England, ordered his feast to be celebrated fittingly, and in 1347 King Edward III named him patron of England. St. George is likewise the patron of other nations, for example, Portugal, Lithuania, and Ethiopia. His memorial is kept on April 23, the date it has always been celebrated in the East.

April 24
St. Fidelis of Sigmaringen, Priest and Martyr

St. Fidelis was born in Sigmaringen, Germany, in October 1578. His true name, however, was Mark Roy. He earned a degree in philosophy from Freiburg im Breisgau in 1603, and then spent several years (1604-1610) as a tutor for the sons of German nobility, taking them on educational tours of France, Italy, and Spain. He resumed (1610) his studies and earned a law degree (1611). He practiced law in Esisheim until 1612, when he decided to become a priest. He subsequently entered

(October 4, 1612) the Capuchin Order and received the name Fidelis. In 1617 he initiated his career as a preacher, and in 1622 he was in charge of the Capuchin mission in the Rhaetian Alps (Switzerland), and worked under the auspices of the Congregation for the Propagation of the Faith. His preaching among the Grisons, an area which had turned to Protestantism in 1608, was favorably received and several prominent civic leaders were brought back to the Church. He then decided to preach in Seewis, where he was attacked in church and slain on April 24, 1622. St. Fidelis was the first martyr of the Propagation of the Faith and was canonized by Pope Benedict XIV in 1746.

April 25
St. Mark, Evangelist
Feast

St. Mark is the author of the second canonical Gospel and was a member of the first Christian community in Jerusalem. His mother Mary owned the house where the Jerusalem Christians met for prayer and where Peter stayed after he was miraculously liberated from prison (Acts 12:12-17). Mark accompanied Paul and Barnabas on their first missionary journey to Antioch in Syria (Acts 12:25). He was likewise with Paul in Rome (Col. 4:10; Phlm. 24) and was associated with Peter in that same city (1 Pt. 5:13). It was most probably in Rome that Mark wrote his Gospel sometime after Peter's death (about 64) and before the year 70, basing it on Peter's preaching. Tradition has it that Mark subsequently went to Alexandria in Egypt where he was bishop and where he was martyred toward the end of the first century. His relics were taken (828), supposedly to keep them from being profaned by unbelievers, to Venice by two

Venetian merchants. His feast has been celebrated on April 25 from earliest times.

+April 27
St. Peter Canisius, Priest and Doctor
Memorial

St. Peter Canisius was a Dutchman, born in Nijmegen on May 8, 1521. In 1536 he went to study at Cologne, Germany, and there he met Blessed Peter Faber (see August 2), one of St. Ignatius of Loyola's (see July 31) first companions. Peter became (1543) a Jesuit, then went to Rome and from there he was assigned to the Jesuit college in Messina, Sicily. In September 1549 Pope Paul III asked him to return to Germany to defend the Catholic Church against the attacks of the Reformers. He taught at the university in Ingolstadt (Germany), and from the pulpit explained to the faithful the basic teachings of Catholicism. In this way he brought many Catholics back to the faith. He then went to Vienna (1552) and there he did what he had done in Ingolstadt. He also wrote a *Catechism* that was in use up to the nineteenth century. During his years in Germany and Austria he founded eighteen colleges and wrote thirty-eight books, but it was especially through his preaching that he helped restore Catholicism in those countries. He died on December 21, 1597, and was canonized by Pope Pius XI in 1925. In recognition of his writings defending the faith, he was also declared a Doctor of the Church. The opening prayer of today's Mass summarizes his apostolate when it prays for men "like St. Peter Canisius to sow the good seed of your word among the peoples of the world so that they may win them to you."

April 28
St. Peter Chanel, Priest and Martyr

St. Peter Chanel was born in Cuet, France, on July 12, 1803. After his ordination (1827) as a diocesan priest, he thought of becoming a missionary, and with this in mind he entered the Society of Mary (Marist Fathers) in 1831. He left France in 1836 for Western Oceania and arrived on Futuna Island in November 1837. During his three and a half years on the island he struggled with an unknown language, suffered privation and, finally, persecution from the local chiefs. As a missionary he had little success and gained only a few converts to the Church. On April 28, 1841, a group of men came to his hut, and presuming that they wanted to ask him a question, he invited them in. Once in the hut the men clubbed him to death. St. Peter Chanel, Oceania's first martyr, was canonized by Pope Pius XII in 1954.

April 29
St. Catherine of Siena, Virgin and Doctor
Memorial

St. Catherine Benincasa was born in Siena, Italy, about 1347. From her earliest years she enjoyed visions and lived a life of penance. When she was about seventeen she joined (1364/1365) the Third Order of St. Dominic, and because of her reputation for holiness a group of followers soon formed around her. At the request of the city of Florence, she traveled (1376) to Avignon, France, where Pope Gregory XI was then residing, to negotiate peace between the pope and the Florentines. While there she pleaded with the pope to return to Rome, which he did in January 1377. After Pope Gregory's death (March 27, 1378) and the election

(April 8, 1378) of Pope Urban VI and that of the Antipope Clement VII (September 20, 1378), which initiated the Great Schism, Catherine went to Rome and worked to restore the Church's unity. She is also known for her writings, especially her *Dialogues*, which places her among the Church's great spiritual writers. Catherine died in Rome, at age thirty-three, on April 29, 1380. She was canonized by Pope Pius II in 1461, and in 1970 Pope Paul VI declared her a Doctor of the Church. Today's prayer mentions Catherine's "serving the Church," a reference to her influence in convincing the pope to leave Avignon and return to Rome.

April 30
St. Pius V, Pope

St. Pius was born Anthony Ghislieri in Bosco Marengo, near Alessandria in northern Italy, on January 17, 1504. He entered the Dominican Order when he was fourteen and took the name Michael; after his ordination to the priesthood (1528) he taught theology at the Dominican scholasticate in Pavia. In 1551 Pope Julius III appointed him commissary general of the Roman Inquisition; he then became Bishop of Sutri in 1556, cardinal in 1557, and inquisitor general in 1558. Upon the death of Pope Pius IV, he was elected pope on January 7, 1566, and chose the name of Pius. As pontiff he was as ascetical in life as he was in appearance, wholeheartedly devoted to reform, and determined to preserve the integrity of the Catholic faith against the onslaughts of the Reformers. He revised the *Roman Breviary* (1568) as well as the *Roman Missal* (1570), both of which were used until the revisions ordered by Vatican Council II. He died on May 1, 1572, and was canonized by Pope Clement XI in 1712. When the prayer in today's Mass speaks of St. Pius being chosen by God "to protect the faith and to give [Him] more fitting worship," this is an allusion to his determination to keep the faith unadulterated and to his revision of the Church's liturgical books.

May 1
St. Joseph the Worker

Pope Pius XII instituted the feast of St. Joseph the Worker in 1955 and fixed its celebration for May 1. In European countries May 1, or May Day, is a civil holiday honoring the worker and had its origin in communist countries. The celebrations on that day, rather than emphasizing the dignity of the laborer, turned the day into military propaganda. Seeing that human labor was being exploited by atheistic governments, Pope Pius XII felt the need to remind the world of its proper role and God-given dignity. Thus he dedicated May 1 to St. Joseph the Worker, the carpenter of Nazareth and foster-father of our Lord. It was by the daily work of his hands that Joseph provided for Jesus and Mary. Joseph personifies all workers and reminds us that there is dignity in labor; there is a joy coming from our accomplishments and from our being able to support those we love, our families. As Joseph worked to provide for his family, in similar fashion we too work to provide for our families. By taking a secular celebration, and dedicating it to St. Joseph, Pope Pius XII returned dignity to human labor.

May 2
St. Athanasius, Bishop and Doctor
Memorial

St. Athanasius was born in Alexandria, Egypt, about 295. After his ordination as a deacon (318) he became secretary to Bishop Alexander and with him attended the Council of Nicaea (325). Upon the bishop's death, Athanasius was chosen (328) his successor. During his forty-five years as bishop, Athanasius was five times exiled from his see, since he vigorously championed the faith as formulated at Nicaea and fearlessly supported the Church's teaching about the divinity of Christ against the heretical doctrines of the Arians. He was also a prolific writer and many of his books were written during his seventeen years of exile. His writings (theological, apologetical, exegetical) are important for their explanation and defense of the faith, and it is because of these that he is honored as a Doctor of the Church. He died in Alexandria on May 2, 373, and today's prayer reminds us that he was "an outstanding defender of the truth of Christ's divinity."

May 3
Sts. Philip and James, Apostles
Feast

Sts. Philip and James have shared a common feast in the Church since the time when their relics had been placed under the altar of the church dedicated to them (May 1, about 570) in Rome. Philip was a native of Bethsaida in Galilee, and was among Christ's first disciples (John 1:43-44). After Pentecost he preached the gospel in Phrygia and was martyred in Hierapolis. Tradition has it that he was crucified head downward during the persecution of Domitian (emperor 81-96). James was the son of Alphaeus (Matt. 10:3) and a relative of our Lord (Matt. 13:55). He is frequently referred to as "James the Less," to indicate that he was younger than the other apostle who was likewise named James. He is usually identified with the James who became Bishop of Jerusalem (Acts 15), and he is presumed to be the author of one of the New Testament epistles. He too was martyred, but in Jerusalem, about the year 62. He was thrown from a pinnacle of the temple, and then stoned and clubbed to death. The first reading (1 Cor. 15:1-8) in today's Mass recalls the appearance of the Risen Christ to James, and the Gospel reading (John 14:6-14) is Christ's answer to Philip's request: "Lord, show us the Father."

+May 4
Bl. Joseph Mary Rubio, Priest

Bl. Joseph Rubio was born on July 22, 1864, at Dalías, in southern Spain. He was ordained (1887) a diocesan priest and after a few years of parish work was called to Madrid (1890) to teach in the seminary. In 1906, at age 42, he entered the Society of Jesus, and when his Jesuit formation was over he returned (1911) to Madrid and spent the remaining eighteen years of his life doing pastoral work in that city. He had great appeal in the pulpit--his sermons were simple and sincere, but they always touched people's hearts. He was Madrid's favorite confessor: he spent hours each day guiding individuals along the way of perfection. He also promoted vocations and organized groups of ladies, who made altar linens and vestments for poor parishes. Nor did he forget the city's slums; he regularly visited them and preached to the poor. Since no part of Madrid escaped his influence, he came to be known as the "Apostle of Madrid." He died on May 2, 1929 and Pope John Paul II beatified him in 1985. His apostolate in the confessional and to the city's marginalized are referred to in today's opening prayer, where Blessed Joseph is called "minister of reconciliation and a father of the poor."

May 12
Sts. Nereus and Achilleus, Martyrs

Very little is actually known about the two Romans, Nereus and Achilleus, who had been soldiers, and may have been brothers. They were probably martyred toward the end of the third century during the persecution of Diocletian (emperor 284-305). Tradition claims that they were attached to the household of the Roman matron Flavia Domitilla, and when she was banished for being a Christian, Nereus and Achilleus, also Christians, accompanied her to the island of Terracina. Since they persevered in their profession of Christ, they were beheaded, while Flavia Domitilla was burned. The two brothers were buried on the Ardeatine Way; Pope Damasus (366-384) (see December 11) placed a marble inscription over their tomb and in 390 Pope Siricius (384-399) built a church over it. Their memorial is celebrated on this date since this is the date given in the *Hieronymian Martyrology* (about 450).

Same day
St. Pancras, Martyr

St. Pancras died a martyr's death in 304, during the persecution of Diocletian (emperor 284-305). He was beheaded and buried on the Aurelian Way. Because devotion to the martyr was so popular in Rome, Pope Symmachus (498-514) built a church over his tomb. Accounts of Pancras' martyrdom, written many years later and, therefore, somewhat less reliable, claim that he was born in Phrygia and that he had come to Rome with an uncle and there they became Christians. During the Diocletian persecution, rather than deny his newly adopted faith the fourteen-year-old Pancras chose death. The fifth-century *Hieronymian Martyrology* gives May 12 as the date of his martyrdom.

May 14
St. Matthias, Apostle
Feast

St. Matthias was not one of the original twelve apostles, but after Judas' betrayal and death and prior to the Holy Spirit's descent upon the Church at Pentecost, Peter gathered the disciples together in order to choose someone to take Judas' place among the Twelve. Two candidates were proposed, as today's first reading (Acts 1:15-17, 20-26) narrates. "The choice fell to Matthias" (Acts 1:26), and thus he was numbered among the apostles. Other than this single incident in Acts, nothing else is known about Matthias. Some early writers say that he preached the gospel in Palestine, while others maintain that he evangelized Cappadocia or Ethiopia. He is revered as a martyr, but neither the date nor the manner of his martyrdom is known with certainty. The date of May 14 has been chosen for his feast to approach the time between the Ascension and Pentecost, the period during which he was chosen an apostle.

May 15
St. Isidore

The St. Isidore of today's memorial is distinguished from St. Isidore, Archbishop of Seville (see April 4), by referring to him as Isidore "the Laborer" or "the Farmer." He was born in Madrid, Spain, about 1080. Since his parents were extremely poor, he got a job, as soon as he was old enough, as a day laborer, working on the large estate of a Madrid landowner. He remained in that job for the rest of his life. Isidore took his Christian upbringing seriously. Before going to work each morning, he went to church, and while plowing the fields or sowing seed, he continued his prayers. He always thought of others and was ever ready to help them; he was generous to the poor and often shared his meals with them. What was exceptional about his life was that people noticed that Isidore did marvelous things--he performed miracles. He died on May 15, 1130, and after his death miracles continued to occur and in greater number. Even the kings of Spain were the beneficiaries of his intercession, and thus his cause was introduced and eventually he was canonized by Pope Gregory XV in 1622. St. Isidore the Farmer was later made patron of Madrid, and since he is the patron of farmers he was named (1947) patron of the National Catholic Rural Life Conference of the United States.

+May 16
St. Andrew Bobola, Priest and Martyr
Memorial

St. Andrew Bobola, who is one of the patrons of Poland, was born in the Palatinate of Sandomir in 1591, and entered (1611) the Society of Jesus when he was twenty years old. His priestly life was mostly spent in preaching and in pastoral work. In Vilnius (Lithuania) and Warsaw (Poland) he gained a reputation as a preacher. He was also an exemplary pastor, and when assigned to parishes in Eastern Poland his main concern was to recall to the Catholic Church those who had left it because of an earlier lack of Catholic priests in those areas. In May 1657 Cossacks invaded the region where he was working, and unable to persuade him to renounce his Catholicism, they dragged him to Janów where they subjected him to one of the most cruel torments that any of Christ's martyrs ever had to endure. With God's grace he endured them without any sign of weakness and after two hours of brutal torture a blow with a saber brought his passion to an end. He died on May 16, 1657, and was canonized by Pope Pius XI in 1938.

May 18
St. John I, Pope and Martyr

St. John was born in Tuscany, Italy. He was a senior deacon in Rome at the time of his election, and was consecrated pope on August 13, 523. Shortly before John's election, Emperor Justin I (518-527) passed oppressive measures with regard to the Arians in Constantinople; he seized their churches and forced them to become Catholics. Since Theodoric, Ostrogoth King of Italy (493-526), was an Arian, he looked for a way to get Justin to repeal his anti-Arian laws. Theodoric thus summoned Pope John to his palace in Ravenna and compelled him to go Constantinople and tell Justin to cease his harsh treatment of the Arians. Pope John arrived in Constantinople in October or November 525 and was fittingly received as the successor of St. Peter. He informed Justin of Theodoric's wishes, and though Justin agreed to return the seized churches to the Arians, he would not allow the converted Arians to revert to Arianism. When the embassy returned to Ravenna in early May 526, Theodoric, infuriated because he did not get from Justin all that he demanded, imprisoned the pope. Since Pope John was then ill and worn out from the voyage, he died shortly afterwards, on May 18, 526, perhaps also from maltreatment. He was immediately honored as a martyr and his body was taken to Rome and buried in St. Peter's.

May 20
St. Bernardine of Siena, Priest

St. Bernardine, whose family name was Albizzeschi, was born at Massa Marittima, near Siena, Italy, on September 8, 1380. After his studies at the University of Siena, he entered (1402) the Franciscans. He was ordained in 1404, but it was not until 1417 that he became a traveling preacher, a ministry he continued until his death twenty-seven years later. Bernardine was the best known preacher in the Italy of his day. He criss-crossed northern and central Italy and wherever he preached he drew such crowds that the churches were often too small. During the course of his sermons he preached on living honestly and doing penance, against gambling and worldly ostentation, and always included a few sermons on reverencing the Holy Name of Jesus. In 1444, while in the mountainous Abruzzi area of central Italy, he became ill with a fever and was taken to nearby Aquila, where he died on May 20, 1444. He was canonized by Pope Nicholas V in 1450, six years after his death. The prayer in the Mass today makes particular mention of St. Bernardine's "special love of the Holy Name of Jesus."

+May 24
Our Lady of the Wayside

Jesuits have a special devotion to our Lady of the Wayside because the Roman church that once bore that name was the Society's first church and it was there that St. Ignatius of Loyola (see July 31) and the early Jesuits focused their apostolate. When Ignatius and his companions settled (1538) in Rome, there they celebrated Mass, heard confessions, preached, and taught catechism to children. When the pastor of the church witnessed the good that these Jesuits were accomplishing, he too joined them and asked the pope to place the church under the Society's care (1542). The early Jesuits prayed before the image of our Lady in that church, and it was at her altar that many of them pronounced their vows. When that church was replaced by the larger Church of the Gesù, the image of our Lady was placed in the new church in a special chapel, which is still a favorite shrine for Jesuits and Romans. In today's opening prayer we ask that through Mary's intercession, and through our following of Jesus, who is the way, the truth, and the life, we be led to the Father in heaven.

May 25
St. Bede the Venerable, Priest and Doctor

St. Bede was born in northern England, in the Kingdom of Northumbria, about 672/673. In his youth he was entrusted to the Benedictine monasteries at Wearmouth and Jarrow, where he was educated. After his studies he became a monk and taught in the monastery school. He spent much time doing research in the monastery's library and in writing. He produced many theological and exegetical books, but his most outstanding is his *Ecclesiastical History of the English People*, which he completed about 731. This is the most important historical work of that period and is the only source today for the early history of England and of the Church in England. It is because of this invaluable record that he is known as the "Father of English History." He died at the monastery at Jarrow on May 25, 735, and in recognition of his erudition he was immediately referred to as "Venerable," and revered as a saint. In 1899 Pope Leo XIII named him a Doctor of the Church. Today's prayer recalls St. Bede's erudition when it affirms that God has "enlightened [the] Church with the learning of St. Bede," and prays that we may "learn from his wisdom and benefit from his prayers."

Same day
St. Gregory VII, Pope

Prior to becoming pope, St. Gregory worked closely with five other popes. His name was Hildebrand and he was born in Tuscany, Italy, about 1020. He went to Rome where he became a monk. When Pope Gregory VI (1045-1046) was forced into exile (1046), Hildebrand accompanied him to Germany. When Pope Leo IX (1049-1054) was elected, he called Hildebrand to Rome and made him treasurer of the Roman Church. Pope Leo and his successor Pope Victor II (1055-1057) used Hildebrand for special papal missions. He subsequently worked closely with Popes Nicholas II (1058-1061) and Alexander II (1061-1073), and after Alexander's death, he himself was elected pope on April 22, 1073, by popular acclaim. Pope Gregory was a man of exceptional ability and sought to promote reform within the Church and to abolish lay investiture (royal control over the appointment of bishops and abbots). When Emperor Henry IV ignored the pope's orders and appointed bishops, Gregory excommunicated him and would not reconcile him until he had sought absolution. When Henry seized Rome in March 1084, Pope Gregory was forced to go to Salerno, where he died on May 25, 1085. Today's prayer speaks of the courage and the love of justice that distinguished Pope Gregory and, thus, it recalls Gregory's final words: "I have loved justice and despised iniquity, and because of this I die in exile."

Same day
St. Mary Magdalene de Pazzi, Virgin

St. Mary Magdalene de Pazzi was born Catherine de Pazzi in Florence, Italy, on April 2, 1566. She adopted the name Mary Magdalene when she entered the Carmelite convent in 1582. There she lived a contemplative life of prayer and penance, and in return God favored her with remarkable ecstasies, visions, and supernatural gifts. She became mistress of novices in 1598, and then subprioress of the community. About three years before her death she became ill and then bedridden. Though she suffered greatly, her constant prayer was: "Lord, let me live on that I may suffer more!" She died in Florence on May 25, 1607, and was canonized by Pope Clement IX in 1669. The opening prayer of her Mass today recalls her extraordinary mystical gifts, when it says that God filled her "with heavenly gifts and the fire of [His] love."

May 26
St. Philip Neri, Priest
Memorial

St. Philip Neri was a lawyer's son, and was born in Florence, Italy, on July 21, 1515. When seventeen years old he went (1532) to live with an uncle, a merchant, to learn how to become a businessman. But business was not to Philip's liking; he preferred to serve God and after a year with his uncle, he went (1533) to Rome. There he began his studies in philosophy and theology, but after a couple of years he gave them up to spend his time in prayer and in helping the poor, sick, and homeless. In 1548, with some like-minded individuals, he formed the Confraternity of the Most Holy Trinity to see to the needs of Rome's poor and to care for sick pilgrims in Rome. Realizing that he could do more by becoming a priest, he was ordained in 1551. To his regular apostolic work he now added celebrating Masses and hearing confessions, teaching catechism and offering counsel. Then, with his priest friends he founded (1575) the Congregation of the Oratory. Philip was very popular in Rome--there was no one who did not recognize him--and he did so much good that he was called the "Apostle of Rome." After a full apostolic life, he died at age eighty, on May 26, 1595, and was canonized by Pope Gregory XV in 1622.

May 27
St. Augustine of Canterbury, Bishop

St. Augustine of Canterbury is referred to as the "Apostle of England." He was prior of the monastery of St. Andrew in Rome, when Pope Gregory I chose (596) him and thirty monks to evangelize the Anglo-Saxons. Augustine and his group landed in Kent (England), in 597, and since King Ethelbert's wife, Bertha, was a Christian, the king readily permitted them to begin their preaching in his kingdom. The king likewise gave the monks a house and a church in Canterbury. Through Augustine's preaching King Ethelbert became a Catholic (597) as did many of his subjects. Augustine then went to France, where he was ordained a bishop, and on his return to England he established his see at Canterbury, built the first cathedral there, and sent missionaries and bishops to other parts of England. Augustine's ministry in England lasted only seven years; he died on May 26, 604/605. Since he planted the seed of the Church in that country St. Augustine is also called the "Father of the Church in England."

May 31
Visitation
Feast

Immediately after the angel Gabriel had announced to Mary that she was to become the Mother of God, the angel likewise told her that her "kinswoman has conceived a son in her old age" (Luke 1:36). Upon hearing this news, Mary set out to visit her cousin Elizabeth. Today we commemorate that visit and the Gospel (Luke 1:39-56) of today's Mass describes what happened when the cousins met. The feast of the Visitation seems to have first originated within the Franciscan Order, as early as 1263. The feast then spread through Europe. It was extended to the universal Church by Pope Boniface IX in 1390, to obtain Mary's intercession in bringing an end to the Great Schism, which had begun in 1378. In 1969 the date of its celebration was changed from July 2 to May 31, so that the feast of the Visitation may precede the feast of the Birth of John the Baptist, celebrated on June 24, and thus better conform to the New Testament account.

Friday following Second Sunday after Pentecost
Sacred Heart
Solemnity

In the early Middle Ages devotion to the Heart of Jesus was connected with devotion to His Passion--His Heart is the symbol of His redemptive love. Though the devotion was known for centuries, it only became widespread in France through the zealous preaching and admirable writings of St. John Eudes (see August 19). However, it was first to St. Margaret Mary Alacoque (see October 16) that Christ revealed the treasures of His Sacred Heart and asked that a feast be celebrated in Its honor. When these revelations became public, the devotion became popular for it now took on specific devotional practices, such as that of the First Fridays and reparation to the Sacred Heart. Blessed Claude La Colombière (see February 15) worked with St. Margaret Mary in trying to get such a feast approved in the Church. It was in 1765 that Pope Clement XIII first allowed such a feast to be celebrated in Poland and at the Archconfraternity of the Sacred Heart in Rome. Then Pope Pius IX ordered (1856) it to be celebrated throughout the world on the Friday following the Second Sunday after Pentecost, as it is still celebrated. In 1899 Pope Leo XIII consecrated the human race to the Sacred Heart.

Saturday after the Solemnity of the Sacred Heart
Immaculate Heart of Mary

Devotion to the Immaculate Heart of Mary has its roots in the writings of St. John Eudes (1601-1680), who was a staunch promoter of the devotion to the Sacred Hearts of Jesus and Mary. By the beginning of the nineteenth century this devotion was sufficiently widespread in Europe for Pope Pius VII to allow (1805) a feast honoring Mary's Immaculate Heart in those dioceses that chose to celebrate it. Then, when the world was being torn apart by World War II, Pope Pius XII consecrated (December 8, 1942) the human race to the Immaculate Heart of Mary, and in 1944 the same pontiff extended the feast to the universal Church and fixed its celebration for August 22. Since August 22 is now the feast of the Queenship of Mary, the memorial honoring her Immaculate Heart is fittingly celebrated on the day following the solemnity of the Sacred Heart of Jesus.

June 1
St. Justin, Martyr
Memorial

St. Justin was born of Greek parents in Flavia Neapolis (ancient Shechem, Samaria, today's Nablus, Jordan) about the year 100. He was trained in Greek philosophy and was converted to Christianity about 130. He then taught Christian philosophy at Ephesus and in 135 left for Rome, where he opened his own school. About 165, during the reign of Marcus Aurelius (emperor 161-180), he was delated to the city prefect, Rusticus, for being a Christian, and when he refused to sacrifice to idols, he was scourged and beheaded. The date of his martyrdom is unknown but his feast has always been celebrated in the East on June 1. Justin was an outstanding apologist and was the first Christian thinker to try to reconcile the teachings of faith with reason. The prayer in today's Mass hints that by setting aside his pagan philosophy St. Justin rejected falsehood and chose "the sublime wisdom of Jesus Christ."

June 2
Sts. Marcellinus and Peter, Martyrs

Sts. Marcellinus and Peter were Romans. The former was a priest and the later an exorcist, and they both were martyred about the year 303/304, during the persecution under Diocletian (emperor 284-305). The tradition with regard to their martyrdom is as follows:

Marcellinus and Peter were taken to a wood outside Rome--so that their place of burial would remain unknown--and were beheaded after they had dug their own graves. After their executioner had become a Christian, he revealed the place of burial and the bodies of the martyrs were then placed in a crypt on Rome's Via Labicana. Constantine (emperor 306-337) subsequently erected a church over their crypt and Pope Vigilius (537-555) added their names to the Roman Canon. The *Hieronymian Martyrology* (about 450) gives June 2 as the date of their martyrdom.

June 3
Sts. Charles Lwanga and Companions, Martyrs
Memorial

Today we commemorate the twenty-two canonized martyrs of Uganda, who died between the years 1885-1887. Charles Lwanga was born in Buddu County, Uganda, about 1860. Having learned about the Catholic faith from converts, he also took instructions in the faith. While still a catechumen, he was given a position (1884) in the household of Mtesa, Kabaka (ruler) of Buganda (now part of modern Uganda), as assistant to the one in charge of the boy pages. Months after Mwanga had succeeded (October 1884) his father as ruler, Mwanga's attitude toward Catholics changed. Charles now had to protect his pages from the ruler's perverted demands. Fearing that death may come to them at any moment, Charles (who had been baptized in November 1885) baptized those whom he had been instructing in the faith. Mwanga then initiated (May 26, 1886) a persecution against "those who pray," that is, Christians, and that same day Charles and his Christian pages were arrested, condemned to death, and forced to march to Namugongo, about thirty miles distant. There they were martyred by slow fire on June 3, 1886. Charles Lwanga, his twelve pages, and nine others who met death before or after June 3, were canonized by Pope Paul VI in 1964. The prayer over the gifts recalls the courage that St. Charles Lwanga and companions had in choosing death rather than yielding to sin.

June 5
St. Boniface, Bishop and Martyr
Memorial

St. Boniface is the great "Apostle of Germany." His baptismal name was Winfrid and he is said to have been born at Crediton, Devonshire, England, about the year 675. As a youth he was educated by the Benedictines at Exeter and then at Nursling. He entered the Benedictine Order at Nursling, and after ordination was appointed director of the monastery school. In 716 he went as a missionary to Frisia, but since that country was not ready for missionaries he returned to Nursling. In 717 he was elected abbot, but resigned the following year in order to go to Rome to ask the pope for a mission appointment. On May 15, 719, Pope Gregory II assigned him to evangelize the pagan tribes of Germany, and at the same time the pope changed his name from Winfrid to Boniface. Boniface began his evangelization in Thuringia. He was later consecrated a bishop in Rome in 722 and returned to his mission. His thirty-two years as bishop were very successful, especially after he felled the Oak of Thor at Geismar--conversions were numerous, churches multiplied, dioceses established, and bishops appointed. About 747 Pope Zacharias made him Archbishop of Mainz and Primate of Germany. About 754 Boniface resigned his see and returned to the mission in Frisia, but while preparing to administer confirmation at Dokkum (June 5, 754), the town was attacked by pagans who massacred the archbishop and fifty-three others. Both Germany and England immediately acknowledged him a saint, and in 1874 Pius IX extended his feast to the universal Church.

June 6
St. Norbert, Bishop

St. Norbert was born into a noble family in Xanten, Germany, in the year 1080. Though a canon of St. Victor's in Xanten, he led a rather worldly life at the archbishop's court and at that of Emperor Henry V. In 1115, when a bolt of lightning threw him from his horse, he interpreted this as God's way of telling him to change his manner of life. He retired to a quiet place near Xanten, and there lived a life of penance and recollection (1115-1118). During this period he was also ordained a priest (December 1115). He left his solitude three years later and met Pope Gelasius II at Saint-Gilles, in Languedoc, where the pope authorized him to preach wherever he wished. Norbert began his mission as an itinerant preacher in 1119 and travelled through France and parts of Belgium and Germany. In 1121 he established a monastery near Laon in the valley of Prémontré and, hence, his religious community came to be known as the Premonstratensians. Because of Norbert's renown as a preacher, the cathedral chapter at Magdeburg elected (1126) him their archbishop. He was in Magdeburg eight years, but his zeal in reforming the German clergy brought him enemies. He died in Magdeburg on June 6, 1134. In 1582 Pope Gregory XIII approved his cult and permitted a liturgical celebration in his honor among the Premonstratensians. Pope Clement X then extended (1672) it to the universal Church.

June 9
+Bl. Joseph de Anchieta, Priest

Bl. Joseph de Anchieta is Brazil's most famous missionary. He was born on March 19, 1534, at San Cristóbal de la Laguna on Tenerife in the Canary Islands. Two years after entering the Society of Jesus, he was sent (1553) to the missions in Brazil, where for forty-four years he preached God's word to the native population and helped them to better their way of life. From his tiny mission at São Paulo, today's great metropolis developed, and the great city of Rio de Janeiro grew out of the small settlement he founded. He was proficient in the language of the Tupi Indians and since he wrote plays in Tupi and Portuguese for the students in the Jesuit schools in Brazil to perform, he is today acknowledged as the "Father of Brazilian Literature." Throughout his missionary life he had but one principle of action: "Nothing is too arduous that has for its purpose the honor of God and the salvation of souls." Worn out working for the Lord, he died at Reritiba (now named Anchieta) on June 9, 1597, and was beatified by Pope John Paul II in 1980. Today's prayer sums up Bl. Joseph's missionary life: he identified himself with Brazil's native population so that he could give them God's word and thereby lead them to Jesus.

Same day
St. Ephrem, Deacon and Doctor

St. Ephrem is said to have been born of Christian parents in Nisibis, Mesopotamia (modern Nusaybin, Turkey), about the year 306. He was baptized a Christian as a young man and became a teacher in his native city. After the cession of Nisibis to Persia in 363, he moved to Edessa, where he continued to teach. He remained a deacon (ordained about 338) all his life, and to escape episcopal consecration he is supposed to have feigned madness. His writings, written in Syriac, include biblical exegesis, dogmatic tracts, as well as ascetical works. The Syrian Church has always called him the "Harp of the Holy Spirit," not only because of his hymns, which are still used in the Syrian liturgy, but also because many of his other works were written in meter as well. Ephrem had great devotion to our Lady and in his writings he stresses her perfect sinlessness. He died in Edessa on June 9, 373, and Pope Benedict XV gave him the title of Doctor of the Church in 1920. The opening prayer of the Mass today hints at St. Ephrem's poetical talent when it says that "the Holy Spirit inspired the deacon Ephrem to sing the praise of [God's] mysteries."

June 11
St. Barnabas, Apostle
Memorial

Though St. Barnabas is not listed among the twelve apostles, tradition has given him this title because of his commission by the Holy Spirit and his role in the Church's early missionary efforts. Barnabas was a Jew, born in Cyprus; and though his name was Joseph, he is known as Barnabas ("son of encouragement"), the name the other apostles gave him (Acts 4:36). It was Barnabas who first introduced the newly converted Paul to the apostles (Acts 9:27), and it was he whom the Church of Jerusalem sent as official visitor to the Christian community in Antioch (Acts 11:22). Later, Barnabas and Paul were set apart by the Holy Spirit (Acts 13:2) for a special mission to Cyprus, Barnabas' homeland. After attending the Council of Jerusalem (about the year 50), Barnabas returned to Cyprus (Acts

15:39), while Paul went to evangelize other lands. Barnabas is traditionally considered the founder of the Cypriot Church, and is said to have met a martyr's death at Salamis in the year 61. His memorial is celebrated on June 11, the date on which he is honored in the East.

June 13
St. Anthony of Padua, Priest and Doctor
Memorial

St. Anthony, whose baptismal name was Ferdinand, was born in Lisbon, Portugal, on August 15 (?), 1195. As a youth he joined (1210) the Clerks Regular of St. Augustine in Lisbon, but moved by the martyrdom of certain Franciscans in Morocco, and overcome by a desire to be a missionary in Africa, he left the Clerks Regular and entered (1220) the Franciscans, where he received the name Anthony. He then went as a missionary to Morocco, but bad health forced him to leave. The vessel taking him to Portugal was, however, driven off course due to inclement weather, and eventually it found safe harbor in Sicily. Anthony disembarked and made his way to Assisi, the cradle of the Franciscan Order. He was subsequently ordained to the priesthood and because of his special talent for preaching, was assigned to preach against the heretics in northern Italy (1222-1224) and southern France (1224). St. Francis of Assisi (see October 4) appointed him theologian of the Order and he taught the friars in Montpellier, Bologna, and Padua. He was also superior of various communities, but despite these many tasks, he continued his preaching. So active was he that his health weakened and he died at Arcella, near Padua, on June 13, 1231. Less than a year after his death, he was canonized (May 30, 1232) by Pope Gregory IX. The Franciscans always honored St. Anthony as a Doctor of the Church and Pope Pius XII confirmed them in this belief in 1946. Today's prayer in the Mass mentions St. Anthony's ability in preaching and also calls him "a ready helper in time of need"--a reference to our custom of seeking his intercession whenever something is lost.

June 19
St. Romuald, Abbot

St. Romuald, founder of the Camaldolese Order, was born of a noble family in Ravenna, Italy, about 952. After his father had killed a relative in a duel, Romuald went (about 972) to the monastery of St. Apollinare in Classe to do penance for his father's sin. There he became a monk, but seeking a more austere way of life, left (about 974) and became a disciple of the hermit Marinus near Venice. About 978 he and Marinus moved to the Pyrenees and lived as hermits near the Abbey of Cuxa; ten years later Romuald returned to Italy. In 998 Emperor Otto III appointed him abbot of St. Apollinare in Classe, but he resigned within the year to return to his eremitical way of life. During his lifetime he founded various eremitical congregations in northern and central Italy, but the most important was that at Camaldoli (1023) near Arezzo. This monastery later became the motherhouse of the Camaldolese Order. He died at his hermitage in Val di Castro, near Fabriano, Italy, on June 19, 1027, and five years after his death Rome permitted an altar to be erected over his tomb and his feast to be celebrated. The prayer in today's Mass reminds us that through St. Romuald's monasteries he "renewed the life of solitude and prayer" in the Church.

June 21
St. Aloysius Gonzaga, Religious
Memorial

St. Aloysius Gonzaga, the eldest son of the Marquis of Castiglione, was born in Castiglione delle Stiviere, Italy, on March 9, 1568. Since he was heir to the family title, he was educated as befits a nobleman. In 1577 he and his brother were sent to learn the customs of princely life at the Medici court in Florence, but the empty show of Florentine courtly life was not to his liking. In 1581 he and his family traveled with Empress Maria of Austria to Madrid, and while in Spain Aloysius decided to become a Jesuit. When the marquis heard of his son's decision, he became enraged, took (1584) him back to Italy and sent him touring, thus hoping to distract him from his plan. But Aloysius was not one to change his mind and, finally, his father consented. Aloysius relinquished his title in favor of his brother and entered the Society in Rome in 1585. In 1591, when Rome was suffering from a plague, he would walk the streets looking for the sick so that he could carry them to hospitals, where he would wash them and prepare them for the sacraments. Having caught the plague from someone he had helped, he died in Rome on June 21, 1591. He was canonized by Pope Benedict XIII in 1726, and three years later the same pontiff named him the patron of youth, which Pope Pius XI reaffirmed in 1926. The opening prayer of today's Mass recalls St. Aloysius' setting aside of honors, wealth, and the world so that he might seek only God's glory.

June 22
St. Paulinus of Nola, Bishop

St. Paulinus was born Pontius Meropius Anicius Paulinus at Bordeaux (in modern France) about the year 353. He came from a wealthy family, was well educated, had been governor of Campania (about 381), and had married a wealthy Spanish lady. After a successful career he retired from public life and was baptized (389) at Bordeaux; then in 390 he and his wife settled near Barcelona. Upon the death, shortly after birth, of their only child, Paulinus and his wife agreed to adopt an ascetical way of life and, thus, they distributed all their goods to the poor. In 395, at the insistence of the people, Paulinus was ordained a priest; in the following year he and his wife went to Nola (near Naples, Italy) where he devoted his time to promoting the cult of St. Felix of Nola, a holy confessor who, at one time, had Paulinus under his care. About 409 Paulinus was chosen Bishop of Nola, and as bishop he sought to aid pilgrims and alleviate the needs of the poor. He died in Nola on June 22, 431. It is said that he was the first to introduce (about 420) the use of bells in Christian worship. During his life he was in correspondence with the leading churchmen of his time, and his extant poems indicate that he was among the better Christian poets of the fifth century. The opening prayer of today's Mass mentions Paulinus' "love of poverty and concern for his people."

Same day
Sts. John Fisher, Bishop and Martyr, and
Thomas More, Martyr

St. John Fisher, Cardinal Bishop of Rochester, and St. Thomas More, former Lord Chancellor of England, were both martyred in 1535. John Fisher was born in Beverley, Yorkshire, in 1469. He was university trained and had earned a Doctor of Divinity degree in 1501. In 1504 he was chosen chancellor of Cambridge University and was made Bishop of Rochester that same year. When King Henry VIII asked him his opinion with regard to the king's desired divorce from Catherine of Aragon, the bishop maintained that the marriage was valid. This response earned him the king's displeasure, and when Henry attempted to make himself the Supreme Head of the Church in England, Bishop Fisher publicly spoke out (1531) against it. The royal displeasure was now transformed into wrath.

Sir Thomas More also earned the king's displeasure. He was born in London on February 7, 1477, and after studies at Oxford, he did law in London. He was married (1505), and had four children. Since Thomas was a brilliant lawyer, King Henry took him into his service (1518); he knighted him in 1521, and in 1529 made him Lord Chancellor of England. But when it came to the question of King Henry's divorce, Sir Thomas was unable to support him. The day after the English clergy had yielded to the King's demands, Sir Thomas resigned (May 16, 1532) as chancellor and retired from public life.

Since both Bishop Fisher and Sir Thomas refused (April 13, 1534) to take the oath to the new Act of Succession, they were both taken (April 17, 1534) to the Tower of London. When Pope Paul III heard that Bishop Fisher was imprisoned for his fidelity to the Church's teaching, he raised (May 20, 1535) him to the cardinalate. Cardinal Fisher was convicted of treason on June 17, 1535, and executed on June 22. Sir Thomas was convicted of the same on July 1, 1535, and was executed on July 6. They were both canonized by Pope Pius XI in 1935.

June 24
Birth of St. John the Baptist
Solemnity

Our Mass today commemorates the nativity of St. John the Baptist, the precursor of our Lord. John, the son of Elizabeth, a relative of our Lady, and of Zechariah, a priest, was born six months before our Lord. The series of miraculous events connected with John's birth indicate that his was to be no ordinary vocation. The angel Gabriel, having been sent by God, appeared to Zechariah, while he was fulfilling his priestly duties in the Temple, to inform him that his wife Elizabeth, who was both barren and well along in years, was to have a son. When Zechariah expressed his doubt, he suddenly became mute (Luke 1:1-25). Later, when Mary visited Elizabeth, the unborn child in Elizabeth's womb leaped with joy in the presence of his Lord (Luke 1:39-41). And as today's Gospel reading (Luke 1:56-66, 80) narrates, at the child's circumcision Zechariah suddenly regained his voice when he insisted that the child's name was John, the name given him by the angel. John was to be no ordinary saint; he was chosen by God to have a very special place in the role of redemption. It was his task to preach repentance and thus prepare the people for Christ's coming. It is infrequent that the Church in its liturgical calendar celebrates a birthday; there are only three such, that of Christ (December 25), that of our Lady (September 8), and today's, that of John the Baptist. For all other saints, we regularly celebrate the day they died, that is, their birthday in heaven. The three prayers of today's Mass underline St. John's unique role of precursor--he was chosen to prepare the world for the coming of Christ.

June 27
St. Cyril of Alexandria, Bishop and Doctor

St. Cyril was born in Alexandria, Egypt, about the year 382. Very little is known about his early life, except that he studied in Alexandria, and that it was there that he was ordained a priest. When his uncle Theophilus, Patriarch of Alexandria, died, Cyril was chosen to succeed (412) him. Cyril's years as bishop were uneventful until Nestorius became Patriarch of Constantinople in 428. Nestorius refused to use the word *Theotokos* ("God-bearer") with reference to Mary; he denied that Mary was the Mother of God and said that she was merely the mother of the human Christ. But against Nestorius, Cyril correctly maintained: "If Christ is God, and Mary is His mother, then how is she not the mother of God." Cyril then began writing and preaching against Nestorius' teaching, and since this heresy so disturbed the Church in the East, a council was called to meet at Ephesus in June 431. Cyril presided over that council of Catholic bishops and there Nestorius' heretical teaching was condemned and Nestorius himself deposed. Cyril then returned to his see, where he died on June 27, 444. Cyril was the foremost theologian of his day, and his writings on Christ and on Mary's divine maternity remain as valuable today as when first written. Because of these writings and his championing of the faith, he has always been acknowledged as a Doctor of the Church. The opening prayer of today's Mass mentions that St. Cyril "courageously taught that Mary was the Mother of God."

June 28
St. Irenaeus, Bishop and Martyr
Memorial

St. Irenaeus was the first great theologian in the Church. He was born perhaps between the years 130-140, and possibly in Smyrna, Asia Minor. He was a disciple of St. Polycarp (see February 23) in Smyrna, and later studied at Rome. He subsequently went to Gaul and was ordained a priest in Lyons. Representing the Church of Lyons, he made a visit (about 177) to Pope Eleutherius with regard to the Montanist controversy, but while he was in Rome persecution erupted in Lyons and Bishop Pothinus was martyred. Upon Irenaeus' return (about 178) to Lyons, he was chosen to succeed Pothinus. As bishop he sent missionaries to different parts of Gaul and opposed the teachings of the Gnostics; his most famous work *Against Heresies* was directed against them. Another work of his is *Demonstration of the Apostolic Tradition*, in which he defends the fundamental teaching of the Church as being the same as the teaching of the apostles. The tradition in the Church is that Irenaeus died a martyr on this date about the year 202/203. When the opening prayer of today's Mass says that St. Irenaeus upheld God's truth, this is a reference to his writings, through which he sought to foster unity and peace in the Church.

June 29
Sts. Peter and Paul, Apostles
Solemnity

Sts. Peter and Paul enjoy a joint liturgical celebration because both are considered the founders of the Church in Rome. It was to Peter that our Lord gave the duty of caring for His flock, when He said:

"Feed my sheep!" (John 21:15-17). After Pentecost, Peter was the undisputed leader in the Church (cf. Acts 2:14-39), and because he was so prominent among the Christians he was arrested, but he was also miraculously released, as today's first reading tells (Acts 12:1-11). He then departed Jerusalem (Acts 12:17), probably for Antioch (cf. Gal. 2:11-14), and sometime after the year 50 went to Rome, where he was martyred (between 64-67) during the reign of Nero (emperor 54-68). Tradition has it that Peter was crucified upside down (cf. John 21:18-19) in the Circus of Nero and that he was buried on Vatican Hill, not far from the place where he had died. Archeological research has recently confirmed that Peter's tomb is beneath the present St. Peter's in Rome.

Paul, known as the "Apostle of the Gentiles", was undoubtedly the Church's greatest missionary. After his three extensive missionary journeys, covering the years 47-58, he was arrested (Acts 22:24-25) in Jerusalem about the year 58, and taken to Caesarea where he was confined for two years (Acts 23:27). When Governor Festus was about to transfer him to Jerusalem for trial, Paul exercised his right as a Roman citizen and appealed to Caesar (Acts 25:11), that is, he requested that his trial be in Rome. He was subsequently sent to Rome during the winter of 60-61. Though under house arrest (Acts 28:16) during his two years there (61-63), he was still able to receive visitors and preach to them (Acts 28:30-31). He was then set free and he may have returned to visit some of his former missions. He was arrested a second time, again taken to Rome, and like Peter was martyred during the reign of Nero, sometime between the years 64-67. Tradition maintains that Paul was beheaded about three miles from Rome and that his body was then buried on the Ostian way.

When the Christians feared that the tombs of Peter and Paul might be violated during the persecution of

Valerian (emperor 253-259), they secretly moved (June 29, 258) these sacred relics to "The Catacombs," known today as the Catacombs of St. Sebastian. When peace was restored and when the relics were returned to their original tombs, Constantine built (324) basilicas over each of them. Today the magnificent Basilica of St. Peter stands over that of the Prince of the Apostles, and the inspiring Basilica of St. Paul Outside-the-Walls stands over that of the Apostle of the Gentiles.

June 30
First Martyrs of the Church of Rome

On the day following the commemoration of Sts. Peter and Paul, both of whom had died in the persecution under Nero (emperor 54-68), we commemorate the many others who died for the faith (by crucifixion, fire, or exposure to wild beasts) during the same and succeeding persecutions. Since the number and the names of all these are known to God alone, we remember them today as the First Martyrs of the Church of Rome. A large part of Rome had been destroyed by fire (18-24 July, 64) and the Roman historian Tacitus tells us (*Annales* 15, 44, 3) that Nero tried to put the blame on the Christians. He thus initiated a persecution, the first such by a Roman emperor, accusing the Christians of being incendiaries and for being filled with "hatred for the human race." A martyr is a witness; a witness who gives his testimony in blood. But the mere shedding of blood does not make martyrs, it is the reason why they choose to shed their blood. The shed blood, then, is the martyr's testimony that he prefers death to separation from his Lord and Savior.

+July 2
**Sts. Bernardine Realino, John Francis Regis,
Francis Jerome, and Bl. Julian Maunoir and
Anthony Baldinucci, Priests**
Memorial

The three Jesuit saints and the two Jesuit blessed
we commemorate today spent most of their priestly life
traveling through various parts of Italy and France,
preaching parish missions to the faithful. The
inspiration and content of these missions invariably came
from the *Spiritual Exercises* of St. Ignatius of Loyola (see
July 31).

St. Bernardine Realino was an Italian, born at Carpi
on December 1, 1530. He mainly worked in and around
Lecce, in Apulia. He died there on July 2, 1616, and
was canonized by Pope Pius XII in 1947.

St. John Francis Regis was a Frenchman, born at
Fontcouverte on January 31, 1597. His mission area was
southern France. He died at La Louvesc on December
31, 1640, and was canonized by Pope Clement XII in
1737.

St. Francis Jerome, also an Italian, was born at
Grottaglie, near Taranto, on December 17, 1642.
Naples was his mission area for forty years. He died
there on May 11, 1716, and was canonized by Pope
Gregory XVI in 1839.

Bl. Julian Maunoir did missionary work in Brittany
for forty-three years. He was born at Saint-Georges-de-
Reintembault, near Rennes, on October 1, 1606, and
died at Plévin on January 28, 1683. He was beatified by
Pope Pius XII in 1951.

Bl. Anthony Baldinucci, was born in Florence, Italy,
on June 19, 1665, and for twenty years preached his
missions in the cities and towns surrounding Rome. He
died at Pofi on November 7, 1717, and was beatified by
Pope Leo XIII in 1893.

The prayer of the Mass today recalls the journeys that these itinerant preachers made to carry Christ's "Gospel of peace to towns and villages."

**July 3
St. Thomas, Apostle**
Feast

St. Thomas was one of our Lord's twelve apostles (Matt. 10:3), and the name Thomas means "twin," as John twice tells us in his Gospel (11:16; 20:24). It appears, then, that the Gospels only identify him by his nickname, but later writings, known as apocryphal, call him Judas Thomas, or Judas the Twin. That Thomas was courageous in his following of Christ is well brought out in his remark when Jesus spoke about His returning to Judea: "Let us go along with Him and die with Him" (John 11:16). But Thomas is better remembered for the incident related in today's Gospel (John 20:24-29). He may have once been a "doubting" Thomas, but he was transformed into a "believing" Thomas, and it was this "believing" Thomas who, after Pentecost, became a missionary and evangelized the lands between the Caspian Sea and the Persian Gulf. There is also a tradition that he traveled as far as India, where he preached and died a martyr's death. He is said to have been buried at Mylapore, near Madras, India. The St. Thomas Christians along India's Malabar coast claim him as the founder of their church. His feast is celebrated today because this is the day when the Malabar Christians celebrate it, and thus we join with them in honoring St. Thomas. The prayer after Communion today echoes St. Thomas' unforgettable confession of Christ's divinity when he saw his risen Lord for the first time.

July 4
St. Elizabeth of Portugal

St. Elizabeth, the daughter of Peter III, King of Aragon, was probably born in Saragossa, about the year 1270, and at her baptism she was given the name of her great aunt, St. Elizabeth of Hungary (see November 17), who had been canonized thirty-five years previously. As a young girl Elizabeth was married (1282) to Denis, King of Portugal, and though she bore him two children the marriage was not a happy one. With great patience she endured her husband's infidelities, and with great love she raised his illegitimate children as her own. As Queen of Portugal she was devoted to her people's welfare and was most generous to the poor; she likewise founded hospitals and convents. She was also a peacemaker: she reconciled her husband with their rebellious son Alfonso, and on two occasions averted war between the kings of Aragon and Castile. After her husband's death in 1325, she sold her jewels and possessions, gave the money to the poor, and became a Franciscan tertiary, living near the convent of the Poor Clares in Coimbra. She died at the royal castle in Estremoz, Portugal, on July 4, 1336, while attempting to make peace between her son, Alfonso IV of Portugal, and her nephew, Alfonso XI of Castile. St. Elizabeth was canonized by Pope Urban VIII in 1625. Today's prayer recalls her peacemaking measures when it affirms that God, the "Father of peace and love ... gave St. Elizabeth the gift of reconciling enemies."

July 5
St. Anthony Zaccaria, Priest

St. Anthony Zaccaria was born in Cremona, Italy, in 1502. He studied medicine and graduated from the

University of Padua in 1524. He then returned to Cremona and rather than practicing medicine he devoted his life to the religious apostolate. Thereupon, he taught catechism in a church near his home, and studied for the priesthood; he was ordained in 1528. Two years later (1530) he was sent to Milan to be chaplain to Countess Torelli of Guastalla, and while in Milan he joined the Oratory of Eternal Wisdom. Soon, he and two friends, began laying the foundations for a new congregation of priests, the Clerks Regular of St. Paul, more commonly known as Barnabites because their first church in Milan was that of St. Barnabas. The purpose of this new congregation was to reform sixteenth-century society by preaching, practicing penance, and giving parish missions. St. Anthony himself traveled through Lombardy and the Veneto preaching missions among the people. While on a visit to his mother in Cremona, he died on July 5, 1539, a result of overwork. He was canonized by Pope Leo XIII in 1897. The opening prayer in the Mass today tells us that when St. Anthony Zaccaria founded his congregation to preach Christ's message of salvation, he was following in the spirit of St. Paul, after whom he had named his religious family.

July 6
St. Maria Goretti, Virgin and Martyr

When St. Maria Goretti died a martyr's death to preserve her purity, she was not yet twelve years old. She was born at Corinaldo, near Ancona, Italy, on October 16, 1890. Since her father was unable to find suitable employment, the family twice moved, the last time in 1899 to Ferriere di Conca, about six miles from Nettuno. There the father became a tenant farmer. Because the family was extremely poor, Maria never went to school. Her father died in 1900, and while her mother spent her days working in the fields, Maria cared for the house as well as for her five brothers and sisters. A young lad, in his late teens and who lived next door, became interested in Maria and twice tried to seduce her. But Maria declined his advances, and to make sure that she would not speak of this to his or her mother, he threatened to kill her. Then on July 5, 1902, while Maria's mother was at work, the youth, carrying a dagger, entered the Goretti house. Maria, who had just made her First Communion six weeks before, again repulsed him saying: "No, God does not want it. If you do this, you will go to hell for it." The angry youth then stabbed her a dozen times. Maria died in the hospital at Nettuno the following day. She was canonized by Pope Pius XII in 1950.

July 11
St. Benedict, Abbot
Memorial

St. Benedict is the Patriarch of Western Monasticism. He was born in Nursia, Italy, in the year 480, and since his family was a distinguished one, he studied in Rome. The worldly ways of Rome, however, did not appeal to him and, thus, he donned (about 500) a monastic habit and went to live as a hermit in a grotto near Subiaco. After a few years, disciples joined him and not long afterwards he built twelve monasteries, of twelve monks each, in the immediate vicinity. Because of friction and jealousy arising among the local clergy, Benedict and a group of monks left the Subiaco area, about the year 525, and went further south to Monte Cassino where they built a new monastery among the woods and groves. It was at Monte Cassino that Benedict wrote the *Rule* for his monks, and it was there that he died about 546 or a bit later. He was buried next to his sister Scholastica (see February 10), who had died earlier. By the eighth century, the monks at Monte Cassino celebrated the feast of their founder on July 11. When the opening prayer of today's Mass speaks of "preferring [God's] love to everything else," it echoes Benedict's rule, where he tells his monks "to put nothing before the love of Christ" (chap. 4, 21).

July 13
St. Henry

St. Henry is known in history as Henry II, Holy Roman Emperor. He was born near Hildesheim on May 6, 973, the son of Henry "the Wrangler", Duke of Bavaria. He was educated at Hildesheim and in 995 he succeeded his father. Then in 998 he married Kunegunde, daughter of the Count of Luxembourg. Upon the death of Emperor Otto III in 1002, Henry was elected King of Germany and throughout his years as king, he worked for a lasting peace in Germany, and desired that only suitable and capable bishops be appointed in the Church, and that the clergy and monks live up to their calling. His concern for the Church and its reform flowed from his own devout disposition. During his second visit to Rome, when he intervened to quell a disturbance in the city, Pope Benedict VIII crowned (February 14, 1014) him Holy Roman Emperor. About 1007 Henry founded the see of Bamberg, and with his wife, richly endowed it. He died at Grona, near Göttingen, on July 13, 1024, and was buried in the cathedral at Bamberg. During life and after death, he was revered for his piety and asceticism. He was canonized by Pope Eugene III in 1146, and his wife Kunegunde was canonized by Pope Innocent III in

1200. During the Middle Ages St. Henry was looked upon as the ideal Christian ruler.

July 14
Bl. Kateri Tekakwitha, Virgin
Memorial

Bl. Kateri, the daughter of a Christian Algonquin mother, who had been taken captive by the Mohawk Indians, and of a pagan Mohawk father, was born at Ossernenon (today's Auriesville, New York) in April 1656. Since she was born at sunrise, she was given the name Ioragade ("Sunshine"). As a result of a smallpox epidemic (1659), she lost her parents, and was subsequently brought up by an aunt. Because her vision had been weakened by the disease and because she found it necessary to walk with her hands extended in front of her, her uncle gave her the name Tekakwitha ("who stretches out her hands"). Kateri remembered the rudiments of the Catholic faith that her mother had instilled in her, and when Jesuit missionaries visited the camp in 1667, she hesitated, in her shyness, to ask about the God whom her mother had worshiped. It was only in 1675 that she asked the missionary, who then resided at the camp, to become a Christian. She was baptized on Easter Sunday, April 5, 1676, and was given the name of Kateri or Catherine. Since she was harshly treated by her aunt and uncle because of her conversion, the missionary suggested that she secretly go to the Indian settlement at Caughnawaga, near Montreal, where other Catholic Mohawks were then living. She arrived there in October 1677, and made her First Communion that Christmas. Her three years there were years of peace; she prayed and she cared for the sick and elderly. Due to her excessive penances, her health failed and she died at Caughnawaga on April 17, 1680. She was beatified by

Pope John Paul II in 1980. The monument, which marks the site of her original tomb, bears the inscription: "the most beautiful flower that blossomed."

Same day
St. Camillus de Lellis, Priest

St. Camillus de Lellis was born at Bucchianico, Italy, on May 25, 1550. As a young man he thought of enrolling in the military, but an ulcer on his right foot kept him from fulfilling that desire. He went (1571) to Rome's hospital of San Giacomo for treatment, and after the wound healed he found employment at the hospital as a servant. His service, however, did not last long because he was dismissed for gambling. He then served in the Venetian army for four years (1571-1574), and when he gambled away all that he owned he got a job as a laborer at a Capuchin monastery in Manfredonia (Apulia). Repenting his past life and undergoing a conversion, he joined (1275) the Capuchins as a coadjutor brother. Since the wound became ulcerated once more, he left the Capuchins and returned to the hospital in Rome. Healed, he remained at the hospital for almost three years working with the sick. He then reentered (1579) the Capuchins, but again his wound opened and he was forced to leave. Camillus now decided to dedicate his life to the sick. He returned to San Giacomo and there they asked him to serve as the hospital's superintendent. Coming under the influence of St. Philip Neri (see May 26), he began studies for the priesthood and was ordained in 1584. He gathered others about him who also wanted to share his work, and they called themselves "Servants of the Sick." They daily visited Rome's Santo Spirito hospital and there they nursed the sick, offering them both physical and spiritual assistance, especially in cases near death.

Renowned for his charity, Camillus died in Rome on July 14, 1614, and was canonized by Pope Benedict XIV in 1746. The congregation he founded is called the Order of the Servants of the Sick, but its members are commonly known as Camillians. In 1886 Pope Leo XIII named St. Camillus de Lellis and St. John of God (see March 8) patrons of the sick and of hospitals, and in 1930 Pope Pius XI named St. Camillus patron of nurses. Today's Mass prayer also mentions St. Camillus' "special love for the sick."

July 15
St. Bonaventure, Bishop and Doctor
Memorial

St. Bonaventure's baptismal name was John, but he received the name Bonaventure when he became a Franciscan. He was born at Bagnoregio, near Viterbo, Italy, about 1217. He studied in Paris, and having become acquainted with the Franciscans there he entered their monastery (about 1243) in Paris. He subsequently received his degree from the University of Paris and taught there from 1248 to 1255. In 1257 he was elected superior general of the Franciscans, and the remaining years of his life were spent writing and traveling in behalf of his Order. In 1273 Pope Gregory X made him Cardinal Bishop of Albano, and since the Second Council of Lyons was soon to begin, Bonaventure traveled with Pope Gregory to Lyons, where he was consecrated bishop (November 11/12, 1273). There Bonaventure helped the pope prepare for the council. He died at Lyons on July 15, 1274, and was canonized by Pope Sixtus IV in 1482. In 1588 Pope Sixtus V declared him a Doctor of the Church. St. Bonaventure was the outstanding Franciscan theologian during the Middle Ages, and is especially celebrated for his treatises in mystical theology.

July 16
Our Lady of Mount Carmel

The feast of Our Lady of Mount Carmel was instituted by the Carmelites (Order of Friars of the Blessed Virgin Mary of Mount Carmel) between the years 1376 and 1386, to celebrate Pope Honorius III's approbation of their Order in 1226. The Carmelites chose to celebrate the feast on July 16, the traditional date, when our Lady appeared (1251) in a vision to St. Simon Stock, the sixth general of the Order, and gave him the Carmelite scapular. At that time our Lady also directed him to start a confraternity and promised that anyone wearing the scapular would enjoy her special protection. When the use of the scapular became popular in Europe, Pope Benedict XIII added (1726) the feast to the Roman calendar.

July 21
St. Lawrence of Brindisi, Priest and Doctor

St. Lawrence's true name was Julius Caesar Russo. He was born in Brindisi, southern Italy, on July 22, 1559. After his parents' death he went to Venice and then entered (1575) the Capuchin Order and received the name Lawrence. He studied at Padua and Venice, and during those years his remarkable ability for languages became evident; he was able to speak and preach in at least a half dozen of them. After his ordination in 1582 he was assigned to preaching, his most characteristic apostolate, and he traveled throughout northern Italy and beyond the Alps evangelizing the people. He likewise spent time (1599-1602, 1606-1613) in Bohemia, Germany, Austria, and Hungary working to win back those who had gone over to the Reformation. Within his Order he held many positions of authority, and in 1602 he was chosen superior general. He also engaged in diplomacy; he served as special papal emissary, and in 1614 he made peace between Spain and Savoy, and late in his life the city of Naples, suffering under the oppressive measures of its viceroy, asked him to represent its case before Philip III of Spain. He found the king in Lisbon and won not only a hearing but also a favorable reply. While in Lisbon, he fell ill and died there on July 22, 1619. He was canonized by Pope Leo XIII in 1881, and Pope John XXIII named him a Doctor of the Church in 1959. When today's prayer says that God gave St. Lawrence "courage and right judgment," the courage refers to his fearlessness during many years of preaching in non-Catholic lands, and the judgment to his years as a religious superior and his diplomatic missions.

July 22
St. Mary Magdalene
Memorial

St. Mary Magdalene was a native of Magdala, which was once a town on the western shore of the Sea of Galilee. Luke introduces her in his Gospel as the one "from whom seven devils had gone out" and as one of those who "were assisting [Jesus and the apostles] out of their means" (Luke 8:2). She witnessed our Lord's crucifixion and valiantly stood beneath His cross (John 19:25), and as today's Gospel reading (John 20:1-2, 11-18) narrates, she was the first to see the empty tomb and the resurrected Lord. Tradition sometimes identifies Mary Magdalene, though it is not absolutely clear in the Gospels nor universally held, with Mary, the sister of Martha (Luke 10:39), or the unnamed sinner who entered the house of Simon the Pharisee and wiped our Lord's feet with her hair (Luke 7:37). Today's Mass formula says nothing about Mary Magdalene having been a sinner (as the Mass formula prior to the 1969 liturgical changes had done), rather it stresses that it was she who first saw the risen Jesus and was given the commission to be the messenger of Paschal joy to the apostles. The tradition in the East is that she went to Ephesus with St. John and there she died; by the tenth century her feast was celebrated in Constantinople on July 22. Two texts are proposed for the first reading: the one from the Song of Songs (3:1-4) recalls Mary Magdalene's search for Jesus in the sepulcher, and that from 2 Corinthians (5:14-17) recalls the love that burned within her.

July 23
St. Bridget, Religious

St. Bridget, is the patron saint of Sweden, and was born of an aristocratic family at Finstad about 1302/1303. Her father was the governor of the province of Uppland. When she was about fourteen, she was married (1316) to Ulf Gudmarsson, and of that union four sons and four daughters were born. In 1335 she was invited to the court of King Magnus II to serve as principal lady-in-waiting to Queen Blanche, and she remained there for two years. After her husband's death in 1344, she lived as a penitent near the Cistercian monastery at Alvastra, and during this period her visions and revelations, which began in her youth, became more frequent, and she began to record them in writing. About 1346 she made the first plans for a new religious congregation, the Order of the Most Holy Savior, more commonly known as Brigittines, after its foundress. The new congregation was established to initiate reform in the monastic life and to promote devotion to Christ's Passion. In 1349 Bridget went to Rome to seek approval of her Order and there she worked for the pope's return from Avignon and cared for the poor and the pilgrims in the city. After a pilgrimage to the Holy Land, she died in Rome on July 23, 1373, and in the following year her daughter, St. Catherine of Sweden, took her body back to Sweden. Throughout her life St. Bridget enjoyed mystical graces and revelations, many of which were connected with our Lord's Passion. These were published in 1492 as *Revelations* and were held in great esteem during the Middle Ages. St. Bridget was canonized by Pope Boniface IX in 1391. The prayer of today's Mass affirms that God "revealed the secrets of heaven" to her while "she meditated on the suffering and death" of our Lord.

July 25
St. James, Apostle
Feast

St. James was born in Galilee, the son of Zebedee and the brother of John (Matt. 4:21). His mother was probably Salome (Mark 15:40 and Matt. 27:56), who may also have been the sister of our Lady (John 19:25). James was a fisherman, as were his father and his brother, and it was while he was preparing his nets that our Lord called him to follow Him (Matt. 4:21-22). Together with Peter and John, he witnessed two important moments in our Lord's life: the transfiguration (Mark 9:2) and the agony in the Garden of Gethsemane (Mark 14:33). Tradition maintains that after Pentecost he evangelized Samaria, Judea, and even traveled as far as Spain. He was arrested and beheaded by order of Herod Agrippa I in the year 44 (Acts 12:1-2). James was the first of the apostles to die for Christ, thereby making good his "We can," when our Lord, in today's Gospel (Matt. 20:20-28), asks him and John: "Can you drink of the cup as I am to drink of?" To distinguish him from the other James, also an apostle, he is often called "the Greater," either to indicate that he was called by our Lord prior to the other, or that he was the elder.

July 26
Sts. Joachim and Ann, Parents of Mary
Memorial

Joachim and Ann are the traditional names given to the parents of the Virgin Mary. These names are not found in the four canonical Gospels, but come from the *Protoevangelium of James* (about 170-180), a second century apocryphal gospel. Inasmuch as Joachim and Ann were chosen by God to be the parents of the immaculate Mother of God, it is not unreasonable to attribute holiness to them as well. Devotion to St. Ann preceded devotion to St. Joachim. By the middle of the sixth century a church was dedicated to St. Ann in Jerusalem, built on the traditional site of her home, and about the same time a church was dedicated to her in Constantinople. Her feast was celebrated in Rome by the eighth century, but it only became popular in Europe with the return of the crusaders, who brought the devotion back home with them. A feast honoring St. Joachim was only first introduced in the fifteenth century. The popularity of devotion to Sts. Joachim and Ann is easily explained by their close connection with Mary, and since they were the grandparents of our Lord, they too should share in being members of the "Holy Family."

July 29
St. Martha
Memorial

Martha lived together with her sister Mary and brother Lazarus in Bethany, a town about two miles distant from Jerusalem. Our Lord loved the three of them very dearly (John 11:5) and often visited their home (Luke 10:38), where Martha, perhaps the elder sister, welcomed Him with her usual gracious hospitality and ministered to His needs, as the second of today's Gospel readings (Luke 10:38-42) narrates. It was, however, at the time of their beloved Lazarus' death, as the first of today's Gospel readings (John 11:19-27) tells, that Martha made her powerful confession of faith in Jesus, a confession very similar to that made by Peter, when he and Christ were near Caesarea Philippi (Matt. 16:16). Our Lord asked her whether she believed if He were "the resurrection and the life," "'Yes, Lord,' she replied, 'I have come to believe that you are the Messiah, the Son of God, who is to come into the world'" (John 11:27). The prayers of the Mass today allude to the service of Christ, a service similar to that which Martha had shown Him.

July 30
St. Peter Chrysologus, Bishop and Doctor

St. Peter Chrysologus was born in Imola, Italy, about the year 400, and about 431 he became Bishop of Ravenna, at that time the imperial capital of the West. He was an acquaintance of Eutyches (371?-455), the originator of the Monophysite heresy, but when Eutyches asked him to speak out in his favor, Peter wrote to him insisting that in the matters of faith it is always necessary to adhere to the teaching of the Bishop of Rome. During his life Peter gained a reputation for being an exceptional preacher, as today's opening Mass prayer affirms, and there are 183 extant sermons attributed to him, many of which deal with Christ's Incarnation. Because of his eloquence he was given the additional name "Chrysologus," or "golden-worded." This epithet first originated in the seventh century and most probably in imitation of the epithet given to St. John Chrysostom, that is, "golden-mouthed." Peter Chrysologus is thought to have died, perhaps at Imola, on July 31, about the year 450. Pope Benedict XIII proclaimed him a Doctor of the Church in 1729.

July 31
St. Ignatius of Loyola, Priest
Founder of the Society of Jesus
+*Solemnity*

St. Ignatius of Loyola was born in his family's castle, near Azpeitia, in Spain's Basque country, sometime before October 23, 1491. As a youth he served (1506?-1517) as page to Juan Velázquez de Cuéllar, King Ferdinand V's chief treasurer, and there he learned his courtly manners. In 1517 he entered the service of the Duke of Nájera, Viceroy of Navarre, and while defending the fortress at Pamplona he was wounded (May 20, 1521) by a canon shot. Convalescence was at Loyola Castle and by reading a life of Christ as well as those of the saints, he experienced a conversion and resolved to visit the Holy Land and serve the Lord. On his way to the Holy Land, he stopped at the Benedictine monastery at Montserrat and there made a night's vigil (March 24-25, 1522) before the Black Madonna. He then went to nearby Manresa and spent some eleven months in prayer and penance. After a brief visit to Rome to request papal approval for his pilgrimage, he left Venice and arrived in Jerusalem on September 4, 1523. Less than a month later, he left to return to Venice; he then made his way to Barcelona to begin his studies "in order to help souls." After studies in Barcelona (1524-1526), Alcalá (1526-1527) and Salamanca (1527) Ignatius went to the University of Paris (1528-1535), and there he gathered about him a group of six like-minded men. On August 15, 1534, in a Montmartre chapel, the small band of seven took a vow to go to Jerusalem within a year after their studies, if this were possible, and work for the conversion of the Turks. After their arrival in Venice (1537), they learned that they could not sail for the Holy Land because of imminent war, hence they went (November 1537) to Rome and offered (November 18-23, 1538) their services to Pope Paul III.

After the first companions decided to form a new religious congregation, their plan received Paul III's approval (September 27, 1540), and thus the Society of Jesus was born. Ignatius was then elected general and accepted the office on April 19, 1541; on April 22, in a ceremony at St. Paul Outside-the-Walls, the seven pronounced their vows as Jesuits. As general of the new Order, Ignatius remained in Rome, wrote its Constitutions and supervised the Society's growth, not only in Italy, but in the other countries of Europe as well. He likewise sent missionaries to India. Because of the excessive penances he practiced while at Manresa, his health had been severely impaired and throughout his life his stomach gave him trouble. St. Ignatius died in Rome on July 31, 1556, and was canonized by Pope Gregory XV on March 12, 1622. His *Spiritual Exercises* had been first approved by Pope Paul III on July 31, 1548, and on July 25, 1922, Pope Pius XI named him heavenly patron of all spiritual exercises.

August 1
St. Alphonsus Liguori, Bishop and Doctor
Memorial

St. Alphonsus Liguori was born into a noble Neapolitan family in the small town of Marianella, Italy, on September 27, 1696. He did law studies (1708-1713) at the University of Naples and graduated--at age sixteen--with a degree in both canon and civil law. He then practiced law for several years, until October 1723, when he set his practice and the world aside and began to study theology. After ordination in 1726, he devoted himself to preaching and hearing confessions. In 1732 he founded a congregation of priests, which came to be known as the Congregation of the Most Holy Redeemer, or more commonly Redemptorists. Recognizing the needs of the people of his time, St. Alphonsus directed his congregation toward preaching, giving missions, and instruction. In this way he hoped to educate the faithful in the faith and win back those who had become lax in their practice of the faith. In 1762 he was appointed Bishop of Sant' Agata dei Goti, and now became interested in the reform of the clergy and upgrading seminaries. In 1768 he was stricken with a rheumatic illness that eventually forced him to resign his see in 1775. He then spent the rest of life supervising the growth of his congregation and writing ascetical and theological books. He is especially famous for his text in moral theology which has been used in seminaries throughout the world. He died at Nocera de' Pagani, near Salerno, on August 1, 1787, and was canonized by Pope Gregory XVI in 1839. In 1871 Pope Pius IX declared him a Doctor of the Church, and in 1950 Pope Pius XII made him patron of moralists and confessors.

August 2
+Bl. Peter Faber, Priest

Bl. Peter Faber was St. Ignatius of Loyola's first recruit. He was born on April 13, 1506, in Villaret, Savoy, and went (1525) to study at the University of Paris, where his roommate was St. Francis Xavier (see December 3), and later St. Ignatius (see July 31). Under the latter's direction, he decided to become a priest and to follow in the footsteps of Christ. On August 15, 1534, he and six companions vowed poverty, chastity, and to go to the Holy Land to convert the Turks. When they arrived in Venice and learned that it was impossible to go to the Holy Land because of war with the Turks, Peter and friends went to Rome and offered (November 1538) their services to Pope Paul III. The pope then appointed him to teach Scripture at Rome's Sapienza College, but in 1540 the pope sent him to Worms and Regensburg to be present at the religious dialogue between Catholics and Protestants. From there he went (1541) to Spain where, by his sermons and missions, he made the young Society of Jesus known. Responding again to a papal order, he went to Germany as assistant to the papal nuncio. Then at the request of King John III of Portugal, he visited Portugal and made plans for the Jesuits to go to that country. Since Pope Paul III had named him one of his theologians at the Council of Trent, Peter traveled to Rome to see Ignatius before making his way to the council. While in Rome he became ill and died on August 1, 1546. Pope Pius IX, acknowledging the cult that had been paid him in his native Savoy, declared, on September 5, 1872, that Peter Faber was among the blessed in heaven.

Same day
St. Eusebius of Vercelli, Bishop

St. Eusebius was born in Sardinia, sometime in the early part of the fourth century. He studied in Rome and there became a priest during the pontificate of Pope Julius I (337-352), and was made Bishop of Vercelli, in Piedmont, Italy, about the year 340. He lived with his priests in community, in a manner similar to that later developed by Canons Regular. Throughout his years as bishop he was a strong opponent of the Arians, who denied Christ's divinity, and because of his firm support of the teachings of St. Athanasius (see May 2) at the Council of Milan in 355, Constantius II (emperor 337-361), who favored the Arians, had him sent into exile to Scythopolis in Palestine (today's Bet She'an, Israel). He was released in 362 after Julian "the Apostate" (emperor 361-363) had come to power, and he returned to his diocese, where he continued, with St. Hilary of Poitiers (see January 13), to oppose the Arians and their heretical doctrines. He died at Vercelli on August 1, 371. The Mass prayer today aptly recalls that "St. Eusebius affirmed the divinity of Christ" in his long conflict with the Arians.

August 4
St. John Vianney, Priest
Memorial

St. John Vianney is better known as the Curé of Ars. He was born at Dardilly, near Lyons, France, on May 8, 1786. Since the years of his growing up coincided with those of the French Revolution and its aftermath, he only had a few months of formal schooling. When he was eighteen, he began, because of the disturbed times, private studies for the priesthood, but such studies were difficult for someone without a proper educational foundation. In 1809 he was called to military service but due to illness he was unable to join his unit before it departed, and later when it was time to join a subsequent unit, he missed it because he visited a church on the way. Trying to catch up with his second unit, he found another young man in a similar situation and followed him; but the young man, rather than looking for the unit, sought asylum in a small village and there they remained until an amnesty was granted in March 1810. John then attended the minor seminary; in 1813 he went to Lyons for theology, but had to leave the following year (1814) because he was unable to cope with Latin. After being privately tutored he was finally ordained in 1815. In 1818 he was assigned to the small parish of Ars--a parish of 230 individuals, all of whom had become slovenly in their practice of religion. He cleaned and restored the church, visited the families in the parish, and began catechism classes. Within eight years what was a dying parish was vibrant with life. Fr. Vianney was known for his ability to read hearts and thus he became a renowned confessor with penitents coming from all parts of France. He spent an average of twelve to thirteen hours a day in the confessional! He died at Ars on August 4, 1859; he had been there forty-one years. He was canonized by Pope Pius XI in 1925, and in 1929 the same pope made him patron of parish priests.

August 5
Dedication of St. Mary Major

Today we commemorate the dedication of the Basilica of St. Mary Major in Rome. Pope Sixtus III (432-440) reconstructed a church previously built by Pope Liberius (352-366) on Rome's Esquiline Hill, and on August 5, as affirmed in the *Hieronymian Martyrology* (about 450), Pope Sixtus had dedicated (434) it to our Lady. The dedication was in memory of the definition of the Council of Ephesus (431) that Mary was indeed *Theotokos*, that is, Mother of God. This may have been the first church dedicated to Mary in Rome. The basilica is now called St. Mary Major, not only because it may be the oldest church honoring our Lady, but it is the largest and most important of all churches dedicated to her. This feast, which was at first only celebrated in Rome, was at one time also known as that of Our Lady of the Snow. A legend, that goes back to the tenth century, says that Pope Liberius built his basilica on the spot where there was a miraculous midsummer snowfall, as our Lady had predicted.

August 6
Transfiguration
Feast

The feast of our Lord's Transfiguration was celebrated in the East as early as the fourth or fifth century. Though the New Testament accounts of the Transfiguration (A: Matt. 17:1-9; B: Mark 9:2-10; C: Luke 9:28-36) do not mention the mountain where this singular event took place, nevertheless, tradition has taken it to be Mount Tabor, about six miles southeast of Nazareth. In the fourth or fifth century a church had been erected there and since it was consecrated on August 6, that date became the day when the feast was usually celebrated. The feast was then introduced in the West in the eighth century, but it remained for a long time only a local Roman celebration. Then on August 6, 1456, news arrived in Rome that the Christian army at Belgrade, on the previous July 22, had been victorious over the Turks. In memory of this victory, and the fact that the news arrived in Rome on the feast of the Transfiguration, Pope Callistus III then added (August 6, 1457) the feast to the Roman calendar so that it could be celebrated throughout the Christian world.

August 7
Sts. Sixtus II, Pope and Martyr
and Companions, Martyrs

St. Sixtus, who may have been of Greek extraction, was elected pope in August 257, at a time when Valerian (emperor 253-259) began a persecution against the Christians. Sixtus met his death after Valerian issued (August 258) his second and more severe edict, which ordered the summary execution of Christian bishops, priests, and deacons. On August 6, 258, Pope Sixtus and his seven deacons were conducting a service in the cemetery of Praetextatus, when imperial police discovered them and beheaded Sixtus and four deacons (Januarius, Magnus, Stephen, and Vincent). Two deacons (Felicissimus and Agapitus) were martyred later that day, while the seventh (Lawrence), was martyred three days later (see August 10). The bodies of Sixtus and the four deacons were buried in the cemetery of Callistus, directly across from the cemetery of Praetextatus, on the Appian Way. Sixtus was one of the most venerated martyrs of the Roman Church and his name was, thus, added to the Roman Canon.

Same day
St. Cajetan, Priest

St. Cajetan, the son of Count Gaspare da Theine, was born in Vicenza, northern Italy, in October 1480.

He pursued law studies at the University of Padua, and after graduation went (1506) to Rome, where Pope Julius II had given him an appointment in the Roman Curia. There he joined the Oratory of Divine Love, a group devoted to piety and charity, and helped at the San Giacomo hospital for incurables. He was ordained in 1516 and was back in Vicenza in 1518, engaged in charitable works. In 1520 he founded a hospital for incurables in Venice. He returned (1523) to Rome, and in 1524 he and three companions founded the Congregation of Clerks Regular, priests dedicated to work for the reform of society according to Christian principles. They were active in Rome until the sack of the city in 1527, then they made their headquarters in Venice. Later in 1533 Cajetan became superior of a new foundation in Naples; he labored there until his death, except for a brief period (1540-1543) when he was superior in Venice. He died in Naples on August 7, 1547, and was canonized by Pope Clement X in 1671. When today's prayer affirms that St. Cajetan imitated "the apostolic way of life," this refers to his founding of a religious congregation intent on seeking the salvation of the neighbor.

August 8
St. Dominic, Priest
Memorial

St. Dominic Guzmán was born in Caleruega, Old Castile, Spain, about the year 1170. After his studies he was appointed (1196) a canon of the cathedral of Osma, and in 1201 was chosen prior of the cathedral community. While on two royal embassies to northern Europe he learned the needs of the Church, especially in the Languedoc region of France, where the Church was severely threatened by the Albigensian heresy. To assist the Church in its grave need Dominic and several other priests were commissioned by Pope Innocent III as itinerant preachers in order to save the faithful from the heretics. Dominic preached throughout southern France for a period of about ten years (1206-1215). Then in 1215 he thought of forming a religious community which would continue this important work, so he and his companions went to Toulouse, and there they formed what eventually came to be known as the Order of Friars Preachers, more commonly called Dominicans. Dominic only had six more years to live, but during that time he saw his Order expand into France and Spain, Italy, Germany, and Poland. And as it grew he did much travelling in order to visit these foundations. In 1221, after participating in the Order's second general chapter, he became ill and died at Bologna on August 6, 1221. He was canonized by Pope Gregory IX in 1234. Today's prayer recalls that during a period of crisis St. Dominic came "to the aid of [the] Church," that is, by his preaching against the heretics and by founding the Order of Friars Preachers.

August 10
St. Lawrence, Deacon and Martyr
Feast

St. Lawrence was one of the seven deacons of the Church of Rome. He was martyred during the persecution of Valerian (emperor 253-259), who in August 258 ordered the execution of Christian bishops, priests, and deacons. While assisting at a liturgical service in the cemetery of Praetextatus, together with Pope Sixtus II and others, he was apprehended and killed (August 10, 258) three days after Pope Sixtus (see August 7) and companions had been martyred. The tradition concerning his death is as follows. Since

Lawrence was in charge of distributing alms to the poor, the prefect of Rome, being in need of money, asked Lawrence to hand over the Church's treasury. In answer to this request, Lawrence assembled the city's poor, to whom he had distributed whatever money the Church had, and said: "These are the treasury of the Church." Thinking he could compel Lawrence to reveal the hiding place, the prefect had him roasted on a gridiron, and thus Lawrence died a martyr's death. He was one of the most popular saints in the early Church, and his name was added to the Roman Canon. During the time of Constantine (emperor 306-337) a chapel was built over his tomb in the cemetery of Cyriaca on the Via Tiburtina, then Pope Pelagius II (579-590) built a basilica, and today there stands that of St. Lawrence Outside-the-Walls, one of Rome's seven principal churches.

August 11
St. Clare, Virgin
Memorial

St. Clare was born in Assisi in 1194, and moved by the teaching and example of Francis of Assisi (see October 4), she determined to follow his manner of life. She divested herself of all her possessions and against her family's wishes went to live in poverty with Francis and his followers. She received the habit from him in March 1212, and set about living a penitential and ascetical life. She was next joined by her sister Agnes; then their mother Ortolana asked to join them and finally their sister Beatrice. For a monastery Francis gave them an old house near the church of San Damiano, a short distance from Assisi, and in 1215 he appointed Clare abbess. From about 1225 until her death, she was almost constantly ill. Through her great devotion to the Holy Eucharist she was successful, in 1243, in preserving her convent and the city of Assisi from raiding Saracens. She died on August 11, 1253, and devotion to her became so widespread that she was canonized two years later, on August 15, 1255, by Pope Alexander IV. Today's prayer reminds us that the love of poverty that Clare lived and had in her heart was inspired by God.

August 13
Sts. Pontian, Pope and Martyr, and
Hippolytus, Priest and Martyr

St. Pontian was a pope and St. Hippolytus an antipope and both became reconciled when they were sent into exile. Toward the end of Pope Callistus' (217-222) term, Hippolytus, who was a man of great learning, did not agree with Pope Callistus' penitential discipline. He thought the pope was much too easy in forgiving sinners, and hence he had his followers elect him antipope. He remained antipope during the following pontificate of Pope Urban I (223-230) and into that of Pope Pontian (230-235). In 235 Maximinus Thrax (emperor 235-238) initiated his persecution by striking against the Church's leaders and thus he exiled both Pontian and Hippolytus to the salt mines of Sardinia. Either on their way to Sardinia, or shortly after arriving there, Pontian and Hippolytus were reconciled. Pontian then abdicated (September 25, 235) as pope, knowing that he could no longer lead the church while in exile. Pontian died in Sardinia in October 235, not long after his arrival, as a result of the harsh treatment to which he had been subjected. Hippolytus died shortly afterwards of the same cause. The Christians in Rome immediately revered both as martyrs, and Pope Fabian (236-250) (see January 20) had their bodies brought to Rome. Pontian was the first martyred pope to be solemnly buried (August 13, 236 or 237) in the crypt of the popes in the cemetery of Callistus, and Hippolytus was fittingly buried in the cemetery on the Via Tiburtina.

August 14
St. Maximilian Mary Kolbe, Priest and Martyr
Memorial

St. Maximilian Kolbe was born at Zdunska-Wola, Poland, on January 8, 1894. His baptismal name was Raymond; Maximilian was the name he received when he entered (1907) the Conventual Franciscan Friars. He did his studies for the priesthood (1912-1919) in Rome and there he organized (1917) the Militia of Mary Immaculate, an association dedicated to promote devotion to the Blessed Virgin. He returned (1919) to Poland and started *Knight of the Immaculate*, a periodical for Militia members. In 1927, he founded, on the outskirts of Warsaw, the City of the Immaculate (Niepokalanów). Upon his being sent (1930) to Japan, he founded a similar community in Nagasaki, and planned on establishing others throughout the world. In 1936 he returned to Poland and became superior of Niepokalanów. During World War II he was arrested by the Nazis on February 17, 1941, and was sent (May 28) to the concentration camp at Auschwitz. Then, one day toward the end of July, because a prisoner had escaped from Fr. Kolbe's block, ten individuals were chosen at random to die in the starvation bunker. Fr. Kolbe was not among the ten. However, when one of chosen ten sighed: "My poor wife, my poor children!" Fr. Kolbe offered to take his place. The offer was accepted. On August 14, when the Nazis needed the cell for more victims, the officer in charge ordered an injection to be given to hasten the death of the four surviving men.

One of these was Fr. Kolbe. He was canonized as a martyr of charity by Pope John Paul II in 1982. Today's Mass prayer mentions St. Maximilian's love for Mary Immaculate and his heroic love of neighbor, a love that inspired him to give his life for another.

August 16
St. Stephen of Hungary

St. Stephen was the first King of Hungary. The son of Géza, Duke of Hungary, he was born at Esztergom about the year 975, and was given the name Vajk. Sometime during his early years (perhaps 985) he and his father were converted to Christianity and baptized; it was then that he received the name Stephen. He married (after 995) Gisela, daughter of the Duke of Bavaria and sister of St. Henry II (see July 13), Holy Roman Emperor. Upon the death of his father in 997, Stephen succeeded to the throne and on Christmas 1000, he was crowned king with a crown that Pope Sylvester II had sent him. Ever since his conversion he was a fervent Christian, and as king he set about christianizing his country. He established ten dioceses, built churches, and promoted the spread of Benedictine monasteries in the land. During his rule the people lived in harmony and the nation prospered. He died at Esztergom on August 15, 1038, and was buried in Székesfehérvár, in the basilica which he had built. He was canonized by Pope Gregory VII in 1083. Hungarian Catholics look upon St. Stephen as the Founder of the Hungarian Church and of the Hungarian state.

August 18
St. Jane Frances de Chantal, Religious

St. Jane Frances de Chantal is the foundress of the Order of the Visitation of Holy Mary. She was born Jane Frances Frémyot, in Dijon, France, on January 23, 1572. When she was twenty-one years old, she married Baron Cristophe de Rabutin-Chantal and the couple had six children. After seven years of marriage, her husband died in a hunting accident, and consequently she took it upon her self to raise and educate her children. In 1604 she met St. Francis de Sales (see January 24), and now that her children were settled in life, she placed herself under his direction and thought of entering the religious life. In 1610 she and St. Francis founded the cloistered Order of the Visitation. Under her guidance, the Order prospered and the number of convents grew. At the time of her death in Moulins on December 13, 1641, there were eighty convents. St. Jane Frances was canonized by Pope Clement XIII in 1767. The prayer in her Mass today recalls that she fulfilled a double vocation, marriage and religious life.

August 19
St. John Eudes, Priest

St. John Eudes was born in Ri, in Normandy, France, on November 14, 1601. During his studies for the priesthood, he entered (1623) the Oratorians and was later ordained in 1625. During the plagues of 1627 and 1631 he selflessly worked among the victims in his own Normandy. Then in 1633 he entered upon his career as a home missioner visiting parishes giving missions. He traveled throughout Normandy and in other areas of northern France. After eight years of such missions, he began (1641) giving conferences to the clergy, but he soon came to realize that the great need was to upgrade the training and education of candidates for the priesthood. With this in mind he left (1643) the Oratorians and with several other priests formed the Congregation of Jesus and Mary, whose specific purpose was to conduct seminaries and work for the continued formation, both spiritual and intellectual, of the clergy. To provide the seminarians with matter for prayer, he wrote many devotional books, and thereby became one of the most read spiritual authors of the seventeenth century. Throughout his life, both in his preaching and in his writing, he promoted devotion to the Sacred Hearts of Jesus and Mary. He died at Caen on August 19, 1680, and was canonized by Pope Pius XI in 1925. The prayer of the Mass today refers to St. John's deep love for the Sacred Heart and his preaching on that Heart.

August 20
St. Bernard, Abbot and Doctor
Memorial

St. Bernard was born into a noble family at Fontaines near Dijon, France, about 1090. In 1112, with thirty other young noblemen--five of whom were his brothers--he entered the Cistercian monastery at Cîteaux, and three years later (1115) the abbot appointed him to found a new monastery, which he did at Clairvaux. With Bernard as abbot, the monastery of Clairvaux became one of the chief monastic centers in Europe, and he became one of the most influential ecclesiastics in the Church. During the period when there was pope and antipope, he persuaded Anacletus II (1130-1138) to submit to Innocent II (1130-1143) and thus he brought the schism to an end. With the election of his former pupil Eugene III (1145-1153) as pope, his

influence increased.   Pope Eugene then (1146)
commissioned Bernard to preach the Second Crusade,
and he spent the years 1146 and 1147 traveling through
France fulfilling the commission.   Within his own
Cistercian Order he was known for his sermons, which
were almost always commentaries on Scripture or the
liturgy. All his writings show a faith inspired by the
most sublime mysticism. It was his saintliness and his
personality that made him influential and popular.
Worn out by austerities and illness, he died in his abbey
at Clairvaux on August 20, 1153, and was canonized by
Pope Alexander III in 1174. In 1830 Pope Pius VIII
declared him a Doctor of the Church. Each of the
prayers in the Mass today has a reference to St.
Bernard's life: he is called "a radiant light," who strove
"to bring harmony" to the Church, and whose "teachings"
can help us to become wise.

August 21
St. Pius X, Pope
Memorial

St. Pius X is known as the "Pope of the Eucharist."
He was born Joseph Melchior Sarto on June 21, 1835,
at Riese in northern Italy. After ecclesiastical studies in
Padua he was ordained in 1858, and then for seventeen
years did pastoral work in parishes in his diocese. In
1875 he was named chancellor of the Treviso diocese
and spiritual director at the major seminary. In 1884
Pope Leo XIII made him Bishop of Mantua, and then
in 1897 the same pontiff named him Patriarch of Venice
and Cardinal. He was elected pope on August 4, 1903,
and during his pontificate he ably fought against the
threats of Modernism, reformed Church music, codified
the Church's Canon law, and promoted devotion to the
Holy Eucharist. His decrees recommended frequent

and even daily Communion (1907), and lowered the age for receiving First Holy Communion (1910). With the outbreak of World War I, his heart was broken, and he died on August 20, 1914. He was canonized by Pope Pius XII in 1954. The prayers over the gifts and after Communion recall St. Pius X's devotion and love of the Eucharist, while the opening prayer quotes his motto as pope: "to make all things new in Christ" (Eph. 1:10).

August 22
Queenship of Mary
Memorial

The feast of the Queenship of Mary dates from October 11, 1954, the date of its institution by Pope Pius XII. The decree for its liturgical celebration may be recent, but the title of Mary as Queen of Heaven is one of her oldest. Mary is Queen because of her divine motherhood and the excellence of her holiness. Since she is the mother of Christ, who is our Lord and King, then she too is our Lady and Queen. But she is also Queen because she is the holiest of creatures, even from the first moment of her conception. She surpasses all the saints in holiness, and being the finest of our race she now reigns over us as our Queen. This feast of the Queenship of Mary is fittingly celebrated on the octave of our Lady's Assumption, thus linking both feasts together. After her arrival into heaven, her Son, who had already granted her other singular privileges, now, in the presence of the angels and saints, gives her a place at His right hand and crowns her Queen of Heaven.

August 23
St. Rose of Lima, Virgin

St. Rose of Lima is the patroness of Peru, South America, and the Philippines. Her name was Isabel de Flores, and she was born in Lima on April 20, 1586. Her father was a Puerto Rican who had come to Peru with the Spanish conquistadores. She received the name Rose when a housemaid, gazing upon her when she was still an infant, remarked: "She's as lovely as a rose." Her mother then decided that Rose would be her daughter's name, and later she was given that name at the time of confirmation. Even as a young girl growing up, Rose was given to austerities: fasting and mortification. Since her parents denied her permission to enter a convent, and since she preferred not to marry, she endured much misunderstanding from her parents and friends. She continued, however, to remain at home, but she lived a secluded life. To do her share in supporting the family, she did needlework and sold flowers that she grew. When she was twenty she joined the Third Order of St. Dominic and converted a little hut in the backyard into a hermitage, where she often went to pray. She also transformed a room in her parents' house into a sort of infirmary, where she cared for destitute children and elderly people. She died on August 24, 1617, at age thirty-one, and was canonized by Pope Clement X in 1671. The Mass prayer today recalls St. Rose's austerity of life and the fervor of her love for God.

August 24
St. Bartholomew, Apostle
Feast

St. Bartholomew was one of the twelve apostles, as the Gospels tell us (Mark 3:18; Matt. 10:3; Luke 6:14).

It is most likely that the Nathanael mentioned in today's Gospel reading (John 1:45-51) is Bartholomew. Why this difference of name? Bartholomew is a not a given first name but a patronymic and means "son of Talamai" and, therefore, Nathanael could be his given name. It was Philip who brought Nathanael Bartholomew to Christ (John 1:45), and at his first meeting with our Lord, Nathanael confessed: "Rabbi, you are the Son of God; you are the king of Israel." Tradition holds that after Pentecost Bartholomew preached in Greater Armenia and it was there, in the city of Albanopolis (today's Derbent, Dagestan), that he was flayed alive and beheaded by order of King Astyages. When today's opening prayer states that St. Bartholomew was "ever loyal to Christ," this is but another way of phrasing what Jesus had remarked about him: "This man is a true Israelite. There is no guile in Him."

August 25
St. Louis

St. Louis is known in history as Louis IX, King of France. He was the son of Louis VIII and was born at Poissy on April 25, 1214. Upon the death of his father in 1226, he became King of France. In 1234 he married Marguerite of Provence, and the royal couple had ten children. Louis was known for his promotion of justice and peace, at home and abroad, and the nation soon learned that the king's piety and goodness were the source of his strength. During an illness in December 1244 Louis promised to go on a crusade. He left in 1248 for Egypt and there captured (1249) the city of Damietta, but because of floods and heat his men were unable to advance, and eventually they were routed in 1250 and Louis himself was taken prisoner. For his freedom and that of his men, Louis surrendered

Damietta and paid a heavy ransom. He then went on to Syria, where he spent four years rebuilding the strongholds still in the hands of the Christians. He was back in France in 1254, but on the occasion of another crusade, he left France on July 1, 1270, and sailed to Tunis, but while there became ill and died on August 25, 1270. Louis embodied the highest and finest ideals of medieval kingship and was a model to his successors. He was canonized by Pope Boniface VIII in 1297.

Same day
St. Joseph Calasanz, Priest

St. Joseph Calasanz, one of the foremost figures in Catholic education, was born at Peralta de la Sal, Spain, on September 11, 1556. He studied at Lérida and Valencia and then was ordained in 1583. In 1592 he went to Rome, where he was tutor to the Colonna family, and engaged in charitable works (helping in hospitals and teaching catechism). Realizing that the poor had no chance of ever becoming educated, he decided to do something for them. Thus, in 1597 he opened the first free school for poor children, where they would learn secular subjects as well as their catechism. There was no problem finding students for such a school, and the schools soon multiplied in number, not only in Rome, but in other cities in Italy, and then into other countries. In 1617 his community of teachers received recognition as a religious congregation, and they called themselves Clerks Regular of the Pious Schools (more commonly, Piarists). However, too rapid a growth of the congregation created problems for the founder and the congregation soon suffered from internal friction. A favorable solution was eventually had, but only after the founder's death. St. Joseph died in Rome on August 25, 1648, and was canonized by

Pope Clement XIII in 1767. In 1948 Pope Pius XII declared him the patron of all Christian schools. St. Joseph Calasanz' special vocation to be a teacher finds mention in today's opening prayer.

August 27
St. Monica
Memorial

St. Monica was probably born in Tagaste, Numidia (today's Souk-Ahras, Algeria), Africa, about the year 331. Though a Christian, she married a pagan, who was eventually converted before his death (371). The couple had three children and of these St. Augustine (see August 28) was the oldest. As any mother, she was interested in her children's careers, but when she saw Augustine living a dissipated and dissolute life, her maternal heart ached. She wept for him and daily prayed for his conversion. After he left (383) Africa to teach in Rome and then in Milan, Monica followed him. In Milan she witnessed Augustine's conversion and baptism (387), and since he was now determined to live a different manner of life, they decided to return to Africa. At the Roman port of Ostia, just days before they were to sail for North Africa, Monica became ill and died (387). Augustine paints a magnificent portrait of his mother in his *Confessions*. Her cult began to develop in the later Middle Ages and it became popular when her relics were moved in 1430 from Ostia to Rome. Her memorial is now fittingly celebrated on the day prior to that of her distinguished son. The opening prayer of today's Mass speaks of the tears St. Monica shed in beseeching God to convert her son.

August 28
St. Augustine, Bishop and Doctor
Memorial

Aurelius Augustine was born in Tagaste, Numidia (today's Souk-Ahras, Algeria), Africa, on November 13, 354. His mother was St. Monica (see August 27), and his father a pagan. He was enrolled among the catechumens as a child, but his baptism was postponed. Nevertheless, he had a Christian upbringing. He did advanced studies in rhetoric at Carthage (371-374), and while there he got into the habit of a disordered and dissolute life. He subsequently opened a school of rhetoric (376-383) in Carthage, but being attracted by the Manichaeans, he joined them and followed their teachings for nine years. When Manichaeism was unable to answer all his questions, he separated from them. In 383 he went to Rome, where he taught rhetoric for a year, and then moved (384) on to Milan, since he had won, through a competition, that city's chair of rhetoric. Professional curiosity then led him to hear Bishop Ambrose's sermons; he not only found them eloquent but soon his heart was touched by what Ambrose said, and subsequently he was converted and baptized by the bishop during the Easter vigil service of April 24-25, 387.

Upon his return to Tagaste, Augustine freed himself of all his possessions and lived as a monk. He was ordained (391) at the request of the people, and eventually became Bishop of Hippo in 395. Augustine was bishop for thirty-five years, and during that time he courageously fought for the faith against a variety of heresies (Manichaeism [388-405], Donatism [394-411], Pelagianism [412-430]). He died at Hippo on August 28, 430. Augustine was an outstanding preacher, perhaps the Church's best; and since he was the most influential theologian in the Western Church, it is but natural that he should be acknowledged as the greatest Doctor of the Latin Church. His writings are many and they have been preserved these many centuries because they have always been deemed important. The most famous of all, perhaps, is his *Confessions*, an autobiography in which he delineates God's working in his soul. The *Confessions* have never gone out of style, nor out of print. When today's opening prayer says "May we thirst for [God] alone," this is reminiscent of Augustine's famous remark "You made us for Yourself and our hearts find no peace until they rest in You" (*Confessions* I, 1).

Same day
Bl. Junípero Serra, Priest

Bl. Junípero Serra was the founder of the Franciscan missions in California. He was born at Petra, Mallorca, on November 24, 1713; his baptismal name was Miguel José, but when he became a Franciscan in 1730, he chose the name Junípero. After his ordination (1738) and earning his degree in theology (1742) he taught (1743-1749) at the Lullian University in Palma. He then sailed (1749) for Mexico and for the next nineteen years he worked in Mexico, first among the Indians in outlying mission stations, then in Mexico City itself, and later in the Spanish missions in Lower California. When Spain began (1769) to move northward into Upper California, Fr. Serra accompanied the expedition and when it reached present-day San Diego, he there founded (July 16, 1769) his first mission. In the following year he founded (June 3, 1770) the mission of San Carlos Borromeo at Monterey-Carmel and made that his headquarters. In all, he established nine missions, and during his lifetime he five times traveled the full length of the missions. He died at

Carmel on August 28, 1784, and was beatified by Pope John Paul II in 1988. The Franciscan missions of California stand today as his monument.

August 29
Beheading of St. John the Baptist, Martyr
Memorial

The nativity of St. John the Baptist is celebrated on June 24, and today we commemorate his martyrdom by beheading. His death is recorded not only in the Gospels, as in today's reading (Mark 6:17-29), but the Jewish historian Josephus also mentions it in his *Antiquities* (15, 8, 2). Though Herod Antipas, Tetrarch of Galilee, regarded John as a just man, nevertheless, when John publicly criticized him for his unlawful marriage to Herodias, his brother's wife, as well as for his other misdeeds, he had John imprisoned (Luke 3:19-20). Josephus also informs us that it was in the fortress of Machaerus, on the east side of the Dead Sea, that John was detained. Herodias had revenge in her heart and waited for the proper moment; it came when her unnamed daughter danced before Herod and his guests. Thus to fulfill a royal whim, he, of whom our Lord said: "history has not known a man born of woman greater than John" (Matt. 11:11), gave his life in final witness. This feast was celebrated in Jerusalem as early as the first part of the fifth century, and it seems to have been celebrated in Rome by the sixth century. That the feast should be celebrated on August 29 is probably due to the fact that a church dedicated to St. John in Sebaste (today's Sivas, Turkey), where his tomb was believed to have been, was dedicated on this day.

September 3
St. Gregory the Great, Pope and Doctor
Memorial

St. Gregory was born in Rome, of a patrician family, about 540. He was educated in law and entered civil service; about 572 he became prefect of Rome. Two years later (about 574) he decided to become a monk and so he converted his house into a monastery. In 579 Pope Pelagius II sent him to Constantinople to be his representative at the Byzantine court. He was recalled to Rome (about 585/586) and then became the pope's adviser. On the death of Pope Pelagius, Gregory was elected his successor and was consecrated on September 3, 590. As pope he sent (596) St. Augustine of Canterbury (see May 27) and forty monks to convert England, and it was he who introduced several changes into the liturgy of the Mass. He was interested in church music and promoted a plain chant that now bears his name. He was also a voluminous writer: many of his homilies have been preserved, but he is best remembered for his *Pastoral Care* (about 591), which details the duties of a bishop toward his flock. Gregory died on March 12, 604, but his memorial is celebrated today, the anniversary of his consecration as pope. His writings were so esteemed over the centuries that he was the most frequently quoted ecclesiastical author during the Middle Ages. Pope Boniface VIII declared him a Doctor of the Church in 1298. He is one of the four "Great Doctors" of the Latin Church.

September 8
Birth of Mary
Feast

The few historical details known about Mary's life are those found in the Gospels, but there is nothing there about Mary's birth or childhood. In fact Mary's first appearance in the Gospels is the scene where the Archangel Gabriel announces that she is to be the Mother of God. When historical details are lacking, tradition and legend willingly fill in the gaps. Tradition claims that Mary was born in Jerusalem, and as early as the fifth century the Jerusalem Church commemorated Mary's birth on September 8. It seems that the commemoration arose in association with the church that was built near the Pool of Bethsaida and dedicated to the Birth of Mary. Tradition also claims that that church had been built on the site of the dwelling of Joachim and Ann, the parents of Mary. Years later the name of the church was changed and since the time of the crusaders it has been known as that of St. Ann. The prayer in today's Mass refers to Mary's birth as "the dawn of our salvation," for with Mary's birth the coming of Christ the Saviour into our world was imminent.

September 9
St. Peter Claver, Priest
Memorial

St. Peter Claver, the future saint of the slave trade, was born at Verdú in Catalonia, Spain, probably on 25 June 1580, and entered the Society of Jesus in 1602. After studies in Barcelona, he went (1605) to the College of Montesión in Palma de Mallorca to study philosophy and there he met the aged brother Alphonsus Rodríguez (see October 31), who encouraged him to be a missionary in the New World and thus become a saint. In 1610 Peter sailed for the missions in South America and was ordained (1616) in Cartagena, Colombia. Cartagena was a prosperous city teeming with merchants; it was also a port of entry for slaves from Western Africa. Peter waited for the slave ships to arrive with their human cargo, and when they did he and his interpreters, all carrying baskets of food, went aboard to greet the slaves. After comforting those on deck, he went down into the stench-filled holds to minister to those who were sick and dying. When the slaves were brought ashore he visited them daily and gave them religious instruction, until they were sold and taken to other parts of South America. Peter said that during his years working among the slaves, he must have baptized 300,000 of them. After a lingering illness he died in Cartagena on September 8, 1654. Pope Leo XIII canonized him in 1888 and in 1896 the same pontiff declared him special patron of missions to the black nations. In today's prayer we ask, in imitation of St. Peter Claver, for the strength "to overcome all racial hatred and to love each other as brothers and sisters."

+September 10
Bl. Francis Gárate, Religious

Bl. Francis Gárate was born on February 3, 1857, in Spain's Basque country, in a tiny hamlet near the castle where St. Ignatius of Loyola (see July 31) was born. He left home when he was fourteen (1871) and began working as a domestic at the Jesuit college at Orduña, and three years later he entered (1874) the Jesuits as a coadjutor brother. He then was appointed (1877) infirmarian at the college at La Guardia, near the Portuguese border, and ten years later he became (1888) doorkeeper at the University of Deusto in Bilbao, and filled that post for forty-one years. There is nothing remarkable in Francis' life, except that everyone took note of his limitless kindness, goodness, humility, and prayerfulness. He became holy through his "enduring fidelity" in serving God, as today's prayer reminds us. He was practically never without a rosary in his hand. He died on September 9, 1929, and was beatified by Pope John Paul II in 1985.

September 13
St. John Chrysostom, Bishop and Doctor
Memorial

St. John Chrysostom was born in Antioch about 347. After his ordination (386) he was assigned to preach; he became an outstanding preacher, and for twelve years he preached regularly to the people of Antioch. His homilies, which were commentaries on the Scriptures, were published, and it is because of these that he was later declared a Doctor of the Church. John was made Bishop of Constantinople in 398, and he immediately instituted much-needed reforms in his diocese, opened hospitals, and saw that the poor were given the help they needed. His honesty and frankness in speaking out against the luxury of the imperial court and its laxity in morals earned him the hatred of the wealthy and influential, and thus he was forced into exile in June 404. He first spent three years at a frontier outpost in Armenia, but because he still exerted influence in Constantinople through his letters, he was moved further away. On his way to his new place of exile, he was forced to walk the entire distance, over mountains, through rain and burning sun. Finally his health broke and he died at Comana in Pontus on September 14, 407. By the sixth century the name "Chrysostom," which is a Greek word meaning "golden-mouthed" and alludes to his eloquence, was added to his Christian name. The prayer in today's Mass also speaks of his eloquence and heroic sufferings.

September 14
Triumph of the Cross
Feast

The basilica built by Constantine on the sites where Christ had died and where He had risen from the dead was dedicated on September 13, 335. By the end of the fourth century it had become customary that on September 14, the day following the anniversary of the dedication of the basilica, the relic of the wood of the true cross was exposed to the faithful for their veneration. This feast quickly spread throughout the Eastern Church and by the seventh century it was also celebrated in Rome. The feast is today called "The Triumph of the Cross," because by the cross Christ redeemed the world. This is the paradox, that the cross, the symbol of humiliation and of death, should become the efficacious sign of liberation and life. Our liturgy today begins with the antiphon exhorting us to "glory in the cross of our Lord Jesus Christ, for He is our salvation, our life and our resurrection."

September 15
Our Lady of Sorrows
Memorial

The memory of the sorrow that our Lady endured standing at the foot of her son's cross, is fittingly celebrated on the day following the feast of the Triumph of the Cross. Devotion to Our Lady of Sorrows arose in the twelfth century, and in 1687 the Order of the

Servants of Mary (Servites), who from their origin had a special devotion to Mary's sorrows, was granted a liturgical feast to be celebrated on the third Sunday in September. Through the preaching of the Servites, the devotion to the Seven Sorrows of Our Lady spread in the Church and the feast was then extended to the universal Church by Pope Pius VII in 1814 to recall the sufferings that the Church and her earthly head had undergone at the hands of Napoleon Bonaparte (the Pope had been held prisoner by Napoleon [1809-1814]), and in thanksgiving to our Lady for her ever-watchful care and by whose intercession the sufferings of the Church had come to an end. Because of Mary's sharing in her son's sufferings on the cross, as today's opening prayer reminds us, she has also been given to us as our mother, as today's Gospel (John 19:25-27) narrates.

September 16
Sts. Cornelius, Pope and Martyr, and
Cyprian, Bishop and Martyr
Memorial

St. Cornelius was a Roman and was elected pope in March 251, but when Gallus (emperor 251-253) began to persecute the Church in 252 he sent Cornelius into exile (June 252) to Centumcellae (today's Civitavecchia, Italy) and there the pope died in June 253. He was soon honored as a martyr.

St. Cyprian was born in Carthage, North Africa, about 210, and was a teacher of rhetoric. After his conversion (about 246) he studied the Scriptures and subsequently became (249) Bishop of Carthage. During Pope Cornelius' dispute in Rome about readmitting those who had denied the faith during times of persecution, Cyprian agreed with the pope that these lapsed should be readmitted to the Church after doing penance, and he wrote letters to Rome giving his reasons in support of Cornelius. During the persecution under Valerian (emperor 253-259) Cyprian was exiled (August 257) to Curubis, on the African coast. He was later brought back to Carthage and beheaded on September 14, 258. Since Cornelius and Cyprian had been friends in life and had worked together for Church unity, the early Christians celebrated their feasts together, as we do today.

September 17
St. Robert Bellarmine, Bishop and Doctor
Memorial

St. Robert Bellarmine was the greatest theologian of his age and an intrepid defender of the Church. He was born on October 4, 1542, in Montepulciano in central Italy. He entered the Society of Jesus in 1560 and did his ecclesiastical studies in Rome, Padua, and Louvain. After his ordination he was appointed (1570) professor of theology at Louvain, and since this was the time when the Reformation doctrines of Luther and Calvin were fast spreading through Europe, he taught his classes with a view to answering the objections the Reformers brought against the Church. In 1577 he was transferred to Rome where he again taught theology; his lectures were eventually published under the title *Controversies*. In 1597 Pope Clement VIII made him his theological adviser, and two years later (1599) a cardinal, and appointed him to serve on several congregations. In 1602 he became Archbishop of Capua, but on the election of Pope Paul V in 1605, he was asked to remain in Rome and again be the pope's adviser. He died on September 17, 1621, and was canonized by Pope Pius XI in 1930. In recognition of his theological writings, Pope Pius XI also declared (1931) him a Doctor of the

Church. The prayer of today's Mass refers to St. Robert's God-given wisdom which he used in defending the faith of the Church.

September 19
St. Januarius, Bishop and Martyr

St. Januarius is the patron of the city of Naples, Italy. Very little is actually known about his life except that he was Bishop of Benevento and that he died a martyr's death in 305, during the persecution of Diocletian (emperor 284-305). Early traditions would have it that he was born in Naples about 270, and that after a period of imprisonment he was thrown to wild beasts in the amphitheater of Pozzuoli, a town near Naples. Since the beasts did not touch him, he was beheaded. His body was buried in the catacombs of Naples, and later, in 1497, it was transferred to the cathedral church of Naples, where he had long been honored as the city's patron saint.

September 20
Sts. Andrew Kim Taegon, Paul Chong and Companions, Martyrs
Memorial

During Pope John Paul II's visit to Korea in September 1984, he canonized 103 Korean Martyrs, who died between the years 1839-1866. The two most famous of these are St. Andrew Kim Taegon and St. Paul Chong. Paul was born of Catholic parents in 1795, and when he was twenty he went to Seoul and, since the city had no priest, tried to rebuild the Catholic Church. He did his utmost to get missionaries to come to Korea, but his many trips to Peking were unsuccessful. He eventually wrote to Rome and in 1831 the Paris Foreign Mission Society was asked to take charge of the Church in Korea. With the coming of missionaries, Paul began to study for the priesthood, but the persecution of 1839 interrupted his plans. He was arrested, tortured, and beheaded on September 22 of that year. Paul's mother and sister were included among those canonized.

Andrew Kim Taegon was born on August 21, 1821, of parents who were converts to the faith. He began (1837) his seminary studies in Macao and was ordained (1845) in Shanghai, the first native Korean to become a Catholic priest. He returned to Korea and tried to arrange for more missionaries to the enter the country by eluding the border patrol. He was arrested (June 5, 1846), and after 3 months of prison was beheaded on September 16, 1846, at the Han River, near Seoul. Andrew's father was included among those canonized.

September 21
St. Matthew, Apostle and Evangelist
Feast

The apostle Matthew was a Galilean and was most probably born in Capernaum. By profession he was a revenue officer or tax collector (Matt. 10:3), and was working at his post when Jesus noticed him and said to him: "Follow me" (Matt. 9:3). The Evangelist Mark refers to him as Levi the son of Alphaeus (Mark 2:14), but since the description of the call of Levi is the same as the description of the call of Matthew, the individual must also be the same. Matthew is likewise an evangelist, and the Gospel he composed was first written in Aramaic. Little is known about his activity after the events of Pentecost, but it is said that his early ministry was in Judea and that he then preached the gospel in Gentile territory. Early ecclesiastical writers do not agree on the lands he evangelized, some say Persia, others Ethiopia, and still others Parthia. The same must be said about his death, some claim that he died a natural death, while others, and this is the more constant tradition in the Church, that he died a martyr's death, though time and place remain unknown. The *Hieronymian Martyrology* (about 450) states that he met his martyrdom on September 21 "in Persia in the town of Tarrium," more correctly in Tarsuana.

September 26
Sts. Cosmas and Damian, Martyrs

There are numerous legends about Sts. Cosmas and Damian, but what is certain is that they suffered martyrdom at Cyr in Syria during the persecution of Diocletian (emperor 284-305), and that a church was erected over the site of their burial. Tradition would have it that Cosmas and Damian were blood brothers, who were physicians, and because they practiced their profession without charging their patients, they were called "silverless." Devotion to these martyrs spread throughout the Church by the end of the fourth century. In Rome Pope Felix IV (526-530) erected a basilica in their honor by converting a temple in the Roman Forum into a Christian church. September 26 is probably the date of the dedication of this Roman basilica, and it was probably at this time that the names of Cosmas and Damian were added to the Roman Canon.

September 27
St. Vincent de Paul, Priest
Memorial

St. Vincent de Paul was born in Gascony, France, in April 1581. Several years after his ordination to the priesthood he moved (1608) to Paris and cared for a parish on the outskirts of the city. About 1615 he decided to devote his entire life to the poor. Two years later he founded the first Confraternity of Charity, an association of women to help the poor and the sick. He then spent the years 1618-1624 preaching missions in country parishes and establishing his Confraternity of Charity in those remote areas. Seeing the good these missions were producing, he founded (1625) the Congregation of the Mission (Vincentians) to evangelize France's poor rural population. He also initiated retreats for the young men soon to be ordained and later founded seminaries to provide adequate training for priests. With St. Louise de Marillac he founded (1633) the Daughters of Charity, and during the Wars of Religion he organized (1639) relief services for the provinces suffering from the war. He died on September 27, 1660, and was canonized by Pope Clement XII in 1737. Few have ever accomplished as much for the poor as did St. Vincent de Paul. The St. Vincent de Paul Societies in our parishes not only bear his name but they continue his work among the poor. The opening prayer of today's Mass speaks of his working for "the well-being of the poor, and the formation of the clergy," two things that were close to St. Vincent de Paul's heart.

September 28
St. Wenceslaus, Martyr

St. Wenceslaus was the son of the Christian Duke Ratislaus of Bohemia and was born at Stochov, near Prague, about 907. After his father's death in 920, Wenceslaus' mother ruled as regent, but because she was sometimes violent and unjust in her dealings with the people, Wenceslaus took over the government about the year 922, when he was fifteen years old. As duke his main concern was peace in the country and the conversion of his subjects to Christianity. Wenceslaus' younger brother Boleslaus grew increasingly discontented since his brother was duke and not he, and so he began to plot against him. Boleslaus invited Wenceslaus to his estate in Stara Boleslav for a banquet, and there early on the morning of September 28, 929, he had Wenceslaus murdered as the latter was on his way to church. Wenceslaus' body was buried in the cathedral of Prague and he was immediately venerated as a martyr and saint. St. Wenceslaus is the patron saint of Czechoslovakia and is the "Good King Wenceslaus" of the popular Christmas carol.

Same day
St. Lawrence Ruiz and Companions, Martyrs

St. Lawrence Ruiz and fifteen others were martyred in Japan, between the years 1633 and 1637. The group includes Asians (nine Japanese and one Filipino) and Europeans (four Spaniards, one Frenchman, one Italian), who at various times and circumstances, spread the Christian faith in the Philippines, Formosa, and Japan. After suffering a variety of tortures, fourteen were put to death by being suspended by the feet and buried to the waist in a pit containing manure; one was burned at the stake and another died in prison as a result of torture. All were either members of the Dominican Order (nine were priests and two were religious) or else associated with it as Dominican tertiaries.

St. Lawrence Ruiz was born in Binondo, Philippines, where he lived with his wife and three children. He had been educated by the Dominicans and was a member of its Confraternity of the Rosary. When the police were searching for him for a now unspecified crime, he joined (1636) a missionary expedition to Japan in order to escape. After being in a Japanese prison for a year, he was suspended over the pit and died on September 19, 1637. St. Lawrence Ruiz and his fifteen companions were canonized by Pope John Paul II in 1987.

September 29
Sts. Michael, Gabriel and Raphael, Archangels
Feast

Of the many angels that make their appearance on the pages of the Old Testament, only three are identified by name, Michael, Gabriel, and Raphael, and only Michael and Gabriel appear in the New Testament. In the Book of Daniel Michael is called "one of the chief princes" (10:13) or "the great prince, guardian of your people" (12:1), and in the New Testament epistle by Jude (9) he is identified as "archangel" and Revelation (12:7) depicts him as leading the good angels in battle against Satan with the result that Satan and his minions lose their place in heaven. Gabriel is likewise mentioned in the Book of Daniel (8:16, 9:21) but he is better known as the divine messenger who announces to Zechariah the birth of John the Baptist (Luke 1:13-20), and to Mary that she is to be the Mother of God (Luke 1:26-37). Raphael, on the other hand, appears only in

the book of Tobit where he says of himself that he is
"one of the seven angels who enter and serve before the
Glory of the Lord" (12:15) and that he was sent by God
to cure Tobit's blindness (12:14) and to guide his son
Tobiah on his journey. The three archangels are now
commemorated together on September 29 because that
was the day, according to the *Hieronymian Martyrology*
(about 450), when the basilica of St. Michael on the
Salarian Way, north of Rome, was dedicated.

September 30
St. Jerome, Priest and Doctor
Memorial

St. Jerome was born in Stridon, Dalmatia, about
345/347. At age twelve he went to Rome to study and
was baptized there when he was about nineteen. He
then went to Trier (in today's Germany) to study
theology, and spent a few years (368-374) in Aquileia
living a quasi-monastic life with friends. He then lived
for two years in the Syrian desert near Aleppo, and
while there he studied Greek and Hebrew. From there
he went to Antioch where he was ordained (379) a
priest. He was back in Rome in 382 and became
secretary to Pope Damasus I (see December 11), who
asked him to revise the Latin version of the Scriptures
that were then in use. When Damasus died, Jerome
left (385) Rome and went to Bethlehem and there
founded a monastery and spent the remainder of his life
writing. Jerome was probably the most learned man of
his age. He published a new Latin translation (the
Vulgate) of the Hebrew Bible--this was his greatest
achievement--as well as many biblical commentaries.
He was the first biblical scholar and his scholarship was
unsurpassed in the early Church. Because of his
immense erudition and his distinguished writing he was,

by the eighth century, honored as a Doctor of the Church. He died in Bethlehem on September 30, 420.

October 1
St. Theresa of the Child Jesus, Virgin
Memorial

St. Theresa of the Child Jesus, commonly known as "the Little Flower," was born Marie Françoise Thérèse Martin in Alençon, France, on January 2, 1873. After her two sisters had entered the cloistered Carmelite convent at Lisieux, she too applied to enter, but since she was only fourteen her entrance was delayed for a year (1888). In the convent she lived a life of humility, simplicity, and trust in God. She was appointed (1893) mistress of novices and held that position for four years. She contracted tuberculosis about eighteen months prior to her death, which occurred on September 30, 1897. Shortly before her death she wrote her autobiography to teach others her "Little Way" of approaching God. Her "Little Way" has nothing extraordinary about it, it is merely fidelity in the observance of the rule and in the performance of one's duties. Without going beyond the common order of things, Theresa achieved sanctity. She was canonized by Pope Pius XI in 1925. The opening prayer of today's Mass also refers to "the way of St. Theresa."

October 2
Guardian Angels
Memorial

It is the teaching of the Church and theologians, and in accordance with what we read in the Old and New Testaments, that the angels, who are divine messengers, exercise a particular care and protection over individuals on earth and aid them in attaining salvation. In Exodus (20:20) the Lord God told Moses "I am sending an angel before you, to guard you on the way and bring you to the place I have prepared," and after the angel had liberated St. Peter from prison, the latter remarked, "Now I know for certain that the Lord has sent his angel to rescue me from Herod's clutches" (Acts 12:11). The final prayer in today's Mass speaks of the angels keeping "us free from danger in this life" and bringing "us to the joy of eternal life." A feast in honor of the Guardian Angels was celebrated in Valencia, Spain, as early as 1411; it then spread through Spain and into France. Pope Paul V introduced it into the Roman Calendar in 1608, and Pope Clement X later set (1670) its celebration for October 2.

+ October 3
St. Francis Borgia, Priest
Memorial

St. Francis Borgia was the son of the Duke of Gandía and was born in the family's palace on October 28, 1510. He was educated as befitted a Spanish nobleman. While at the royal court of his cousin, Emperor Charles V, he married and lived with the imperial family. When Empress Isabella unexpectedly died in May 1539, Francis escorted the body to Granada, but when the coffin was opened for official recognition prior to burial, Francis no longer saw the face of a youthful queen, but one beyond recognition. He exclaimed: "Never again will I serve a master who can die on me." From that day onward he lived a more austere life. When his father died (1543), Francis succeeded him as Fourth Duke of Gandía, and when his wife died in 1546, he decided to become a Jesuit. He was accepted into the Society, but the fact was kept secret until he settled his temporal affairs and arranged marriages for his eight children. He resigned his title in favor of his eldest son, was ordained (1551) a priest, and worked as a Jesuit in Spain and Portugal. In 1565 he was elected the third general of the Society of Jesus, and seven years later died in Rome on September 30, 1572. He was canonized by Pope Clement X in 1671. The opening prayer of today's Mass gives a brief summary of St. Francis' life, when it prays: "Grant through his prayers that all who have died to sin and renounced the world may live for you alone."

October 4
St. Francis of Assisi
Memorial

St. Francis was born in Assisi, in Umbria, Italy, in 1182. His father, Pietro Bernardone, was a wealthy textile merchant, and thus Francis' youth was spent in comfort and fine clothes. Undergoing an interior conversion and choosing to live in accord with the gospel, he left home in February 1209. He lived a life of simplicity, poverty, and humility, and constantly preached about God's love. His joy in following Christ was so evident and attractive that followers soon joined him, and thus he wrote a rule for them. He called his group Friars Minor, but they are better known as Franciscans. In 1212 he founded an Order of nuns, known today as Poor Clares, after St. Clare of Assisi (see August 11). Others also wanted to follow his manner of life--prayer and penance--and for these he established what is known as the Third Order of St. Francis. Francis always remained a deacon--he felt himself unworthy to be ordained a priest. He died in Assisi on October 3, 1226, and was canonized two years later (1228) by Pope Gregory IX. Francis was undoubtedly the most extraordinary saint of the Middle Ages, and is one of the most attractive of saints. Today's opening prayer tells us that St. Francis reflected "the image of Christ, through [his] life of poverty and humility", and asks that we too may imitate "his joyful love."

+October 6
Bl. Diego Aloysius de San Vitores, Priest and Martyr

Bl. Diego de San Vitores, who died a martyr's death on the island of Guam, was born in Burgos, Spain, on November 12, 1627. He became a Jesuit in 1640 and was ordained eleven years later (1651). His dream was always to go to the missions, and in 1659 he was assigned to the mission in the Philippines. Stationed in Manila, he was dean of the university, but at the same time he visited the sick in the hospitals and helped in various parishes. When a mission was opened in the Ladrones (now Marianas), islands about 900 miles northeast of Manila, Fr. San Vitores was chosen to head the mission. He arrived on Guam in June 1668, and after he had evangelized there he preached to the people on the islands of Saipan and Tinian. On April 2, 1672, he went to the village of Tumon, and while there a native, one of his first converts, out of hatred for the faith, struck him with a cutlass and split his head, and then threw his body into the sea. Diego de San Vitores was beatified by Pope John Paul II in 1985.

Same day
St. Bruno, Priest

St. Bruno was born in Cologne, Germany, before 1030. He attended school in Rheims, France, and after ordination taught theology there and subsequently became the school's master (1056). He was appointed chancellor of the diocese of Rheims in 1075, but since he always had a desire to retire from the world, he left there (about 1082) and lived a life of prayer and penance. Seeking still greater solitude he and six companions went (1084) to Grenoble in southern France, and in the valley of Chartreuse laid the foundation of what eventually became the Carthusian Order. In 1090 Pope Urban II, who had been Bruno's student at Rheims, called him to Rome to be his adviser. When the papal court moved to southern Italy, Bruno went with it, and later with the pope's permission he retired into the wilderness of Calabria and there established another monastery. He died at his monastery in La Torre, near Catanzaro (Calabria), on October 6, 1101. In 1514 Pope Leo X granted the Carthusians permission to celebrate a feast in honor of their founder. The prayer of the Mass for today recalls that St. Bruno chose to serve God in solitude.

Same day
Bl. Marie-Rose Durocher, Virgin

Bl. Marie-Rose Durocher is the foundress of the Sisters of the Holy Names of Jesus and Mary. She was born Eulalie-Mélanie Durocher on October 6, 1811, at Saint-Antoine-sur-Richelieu in the province of Quebec, Canada. In 1830, when her brother was named a pastor, she became his housekeeper, and in the parish she organized (1841) the Daughters of Mary, the first such association in Canada. Many towns in Quebec were without schools, and when Bishop Bourget of Montreal was unable to get sisters from France to help in his diocese, he asked (1843) Eulalie, who for years had thought of becoming a sister, if she would help start a religious congregation for the education of children and young girls. She saw this as God's will and agreed; in 1844 the Sisters of the Holy Names of Jesus and Mary came into existence, and Eulalie then chose Marie-Rose as her religious name. She only had five years left to live, but during that brief period she guided her new congregation, which grew and eventually spread into the United States as well. She died at Longueuil (Quebec) on October 6, 1849, and was beatified by Pope John Paul II in 1982.

October 7
Our Lady of the Rosary
Memorial

The origin of the rosary goes back to the thirteenth or fourteenth centuries, and it is a favorite devotion among Catholics because it permits us to meditate on the principal mysteries of our Lord's life, passion, and resurrection. That there should be a Mass to Our Lady of the Rosary is linked with an important historical event. On October 7, 1571, the Christian fleet gained an overwhelming victory over the Turkish fleet at Lepanto. This victory was attributed to the fact that at the time of the battle, Rosary Confraternities in Rome were reciting the rosary asking our Lady's intercession with God in behalf of the Christian navy. To commemorate this victory Pope Pius V instituted (1571) the feast of Our Lady of Victory to be celebrated in the city of Rome, and two years later Pope Gregory XIII changed its name to that of the Most Holy Rosary. Then, in 1716, Pope

Clement XI extended the feast to the universal Church in thanksgiving for another Christian victory (August 5, 1716), also over the Turks, but this time at Petrovaradin, Yugoslavia. This feast was originally celebrated on the first Sunday in October, and only in 1913 was it assigned to October 7, the anniversary of the victory at Lepanto.

October 9
Sts. Denis, Bishop and Martyr, and Companions, Martyrs

St. Denis is regarded as the patron of France and is said to have been the first Bishop of Paris. Whatever is known of his life is known from what St. Gregory of Tours (538-593) wrote in his *History of the Franks*. Denis, and his companions Rusticus, a priest, and Eleutherius, a deacon, were sent from Rome by Pope Fabian (see January 20), about the year 250, to preach the gospel in Gaul. They were beheaded at Montmartre (Mountain of Martyrs) in Paris, during the persecution of Valerian (emperor 253-259) in 258. St. Genevieve built (about 475) a basilica over St. Denis' tomb, and later (624) the Abbey of St. Denis was founded next to the basilica. His relics were transferred to the abbey on October 9. Legend has it that after his martyrdom St. Denis picked up his head and walked with it for two miles, thus indicating where he wanted to be buried.

Same day
St. John Leonardi, Priest

St. John Leonardi was born at Diecimo, near Lucca, Italy, about 1541. He was trained as a pharmacist, but then decided to leave his profession and study for the priesthood. He was ordained in 1571 and immediately began teaching Christian doctrine to children, and when he needed teachers to help him, he trained them as well. Later (1579) he formed a Confraternity of Christian Doctrine. In 1573 he founded a religious congregation now known as Clerks Regular of the Mother of God. In 1603 he co-founded a seminary in Rome for foreign missions. He died in Rome on October 9, 1609, after nursing his brethren during an influenza epidemic, and was canonized by Pope Pius XI in 1938. Today's prayer mentions St. John Leonardi's principal apostolate, namely, that it was through his ministry that God "proclaimed the good news to countless people."

+October 14
+St. John Ogilvie, Priest and Martyr
Memorial

St. John Ogilvie, whose missionary career lasted only eleven months, was born in Scotland in 1579. He was brought up as a Calvinist but became a Catholic when he was about sixteen, while studying at Louvain, Belgium. He entered the Society of Jesus in 1599, and after his ordination (1610) he worked in Rouen, France, and only in 1613 did he return to Scotland. Since those were times when Catholics were persecuted, he entered the country in disguise and made his way to Edinburgh, where he carried on his priestly work. He frequently traveled to Glasgow to minister to the Catholics living there. On October 4, 1614, he was in Glasgow, where he was scheduled to receive five individuals into the Church, one of these, however, betrayed him and he was arrested and taken to prison. He was subsequently interrogated and tortured, but never would he divulge the names of the Catholics who had befriended him or who had attended his services. After five months of imprisonment he was tried on March 10, 1615, because he denied the king's supremacy in religious matters and upheld the pope's spiritual primacy. He was convicted that same day and was hanged that afternoon. Pope Paul VI canonized him in 1976.

Same day
St. Callistus I, Pope and Martyr

St. Callistus was born in Rome, and was most probably a slave. Because of his mishandling of a banking operation, his Christian master had him condemned to the mines of Sardinia (about 186-189). When released he went to live in Anzio. When Zephyrinus became pope in 199, he made Callistus his deacon and appointed him administrator of the cemetery on the Appian Way (known today as the Catacombs of St. Callistus). He succeeded Zephyrinus as pope in 217. During his pontificate the rigorist party accused him of laxity because he readmitted into the church, after doing suitable penance, those who had been guilty of adultery and fornication or who had apostatized in times of persecution. He died on October 14, 222, seemingly in a popular uprising. He was buried in the cemetery of Calepodius on the Aurelian Way, and was venerated as a martyr. His tomb was discovered in 1960 in a crypt built during the pontificate of Julius I (337-352).

October 15
St. Teresa of Jesus, Virgin and Doctor
Memorial

St. Teresa of Jesus was born in Avila, Spain, on March 28, 1515. When she was twenty, she entered the Carmelite convent in her native city. Her first eighteen years as a nun were not extraordinary, but eventually she became filled with the desire to strive for holiness. In addition, she wanted to reinstate the primitive tradition of Carmel--a more austere and penitential form of religious life. God's special graces, including mystical graces, were now more frequent, and because the convent where she lived was unsuitable for her reform movement, she sought permission to open a new one. At first she met with opposition, but permission was granted and in 1562 she moved to her new convent. Her reform quickly spread: new convents were opened and established convents gradually accepted the reform. She died on the night of October 4, 1582 [that very night the new Gregorian Calendar went into effect, hence she died on October 15], while on a visit to a convent in Alba de Tormes. At the request of her spiritual director she wrote an autobiography which describes the working of God in her soul, and for her sisters she wrote *The Way of Perfection* and other books on prayer and the mystical life. She was canonized by Pope Gregory XV in 1622, and because of her writings Pope Paul VI declared (1970) her a Doctor of the Church. Today's prayer states that the Holy Spirit raised up Teresa "to show [the] Church the way to perfection."

October 16
St. Hedwig, Religious

St. Hedwig, Duchess of Silesia, was born in Andechs, Bavaria, about 1174, and was the daughter of Berthold IV, Count of Andechs. While still very young, she was married to Henry I, Duke of Silesia. Seven children were born of their union and she admirably fulfilled the duties of wife and mother. She lived a devout interior life, cared for the poor and sick, and established hospitals. She brought the Franciscans and Dominicans to Silesia, and with her husband she founded and supported several new monasteries. When her husband died in 1238, she retired to the Cistercian convent at Trzebnica, in the province of Wroclaw, Poland, which convent she and her husband had founded and where her daughter Gertrude was abbess. There she died on October 15, 1243. She was canonized by Pope Clement IV in 1267.

Same day
St. Margaret Mary Alacoque, Virgin

St. Margaret Mary was born in Lauthecourt, France, on July 22, 1647, and entered the convent of the Visitation nuns at Paray-le-Monial in 1671. During the years 1673-1675 she was especially favored by God with mystical graces and revelations of the Sacred Heart of Jesus. Answering to our Lord's requests in these revelations, she helped spread devotion to the Sacred Heart, the practice of receiving Holy Communion on the First Fridays, keeping a Holy Hour of reparation, and establishing a special feast of the Sacred Heart. In all these she was aided by her confessor Blessed Claude La Colombière (see February 15). She died on October 17, 1690, and was canonized by Pope Benedict XV in 1920.

October 17
St. Ignatius of Antioch, Bishop and Martyr
Memorial

St. Ignatius was probably born in Syria and as Bishop of Antioch he was the second successor of St. Peter in that city. During a period of persecution under Trajan (emperor 98-117), he was condemned to the wild beasts and sent under guard to Rome. On his journey to Rome he sent seven epistles to the Christians living in various cities. These epistles are important because they are among the first letters we have of a bishop of the early Church, and because of their content. In his letter to the Romans he exhorts them to be faithful to Christ and asks them not to use influence in trying to prevent his martyrdom, because he considers himself the "wheat of God; and I must be ground by the teeth of wild beasts, to become the pure bread of Christ." These words of his are reflected in today's prayer over the gifts. St. Ignatius was martyred in Rome about the year 110. His feast is celebrated today since this is the day it has always been celebrated in Antioch. The *Calendar of Nicomedia* (about 360) gives October 17 as the date of his martyrdom.

October 18
St. Luke, Evangelist
Feast

St. Luke, the evangelist, was born perhaps in Antioch, Syria, of a Greek-speaking pagan family. He was converted to the Christian faith and became a fellow worker of St. Paul. He was likewise a physician, since St. Paul refers to him as "our most dear physician" (Col. 4:14). Luke first met St. Paul at Troas (Acts 16:11), then accompanied him to Jerusalem (Acts 21:17) and remained with him during his imprisonment in Rome (Acts 28:14b-16; 2 Tim. 4:11). He handed down an account of the beginnings of the Church in his *Acts of the Apostles*, and from St. Paul's preaching he compiled the third Gospel. It is uncertain where he went after St. Paul had been martyred in Rome. Tradition has it that he was martyred toward the end of the first century. The prayer of the Mass today is a terse summary of his Gospel.

October 19
Sts. Isaac Jogues and John de Brébeuf, Priests and Martyrs, and Companions, Martyrs
+*Feast*

Today we commemorate the martyrdom of eight French Jesuits, who had come to North America to teach the Iroquois and Huron Indians about God. They were martyred between the years 1642 and 1649--three at Auriesville, New York, and five in Canada.

Martyred at Auriesville, New York

	Birth	**Death**
René Goupil	1608	September 29, 1642
Isaac Jogues	1607	October 18, 1646
John de la Lande	?	October 19, 1646

Martyred in Canada

	Birth	**Death**
Anthony Daniel	1601	July 4, 1648
John de Brébeuf	1593	March 16, 1649
Gabriel Lalemant	1610	March 17, 1649
Charles Garnier	1606	December 7, 1649
Noel Chabanel	1613	December 8, 1649

Goupil, Jogues, la Lande, and Chabanel were tomahawked to death; Daniel and Garnier were shot; Brébeuf and Lalemant were brutally and cruelly tortured to death. Six were priests, Goupil and la Lande were coadjutor brothers. They were canonized by Pope Pius XI in 1930. This morning's opening prayer reminds us that these martyred missionaries "consecrated the first beginnings of the faith in North America" not only by their preaching of God's Word, but also by the shedding of their blood.

Same day
St. Paul of the Cross, Priest

St. Paul of the Cross, founder of the Passionists, was born Paul Francis Danei, in Ovada, Italy, on January 3, 1694. As a young man he led a most spiritual life and worked among the poor. He was ordained in 1727, and because he had such great devotion to Christ's cross, he chose to be known as Paul of the Cross. The congregation of priests that he founded (1728) were dedicated to a life of prayer, penance, and to preaching parish missions. For about thirty years (1730-1760) he himself travelled throughout Italy giving parish missions and emphasizing devotion to our Lord's Passion. In 1771 he founded a contemplative order of Passionist nuns. Throughout his life he was favored with extraordinary mystical graces. He died in Rome on October 18, 1775, and was canonized by Pius IX in 1867. His "special love for the cross of Christ" is mentioned in the opening prayer of today's Mass.

October 23
St. John of Capistrano, Priest

St. John was born at Capistrano, near Aquila, Italy, on June 24, 1386, and had studied law at Perugia. In 1413 he became a member of that city's civic administration. In 1416 he entered the Observant Franciscans and after his ordination (1418) he began his ministry of preaching which took him throughout Italy. In 1452 Pope Nicholas V sent him to Germany and Austria to preach against the followers of John Hus. He likewise preached in Poland, Bohemia, and Moravia. Since Europe was again threatened by the Turks, he preached a crusade (1455) and successfully gathered an army that was placed under the command of the

Hungarian general, Hunyadi. When the city of Belgrade was besieged, St. John took charge of one wing of the army, bravely withstood the Turkish onslaught, and finally gained a victory (July 22, 1456), thus saving the city and Europe from the Turks. He died at Ilok, Yugoslavia, on October 23, 1456. Because of his widespread preaching in Europe he is often called the "Apostle of Europe." Pope Alexander VIII canonized him in 1690. The prayer of today's Mass reminds us that it was through St. John's preaching that God's people found comfort when they had been threatened by the Turks.

October 24
St. Anthony Claret, Bishop

St. Anthony Claret was born in Sallent, Spain, on December 23, 1807. He was the son of a weaver and as a youth he worked in the textile mills of Barcelona. He was ordained in 1835 and carried on his priestly ministry in Catalonia and the Canary Islands. By 1840 he became one of the country's most popular preachers, and in 1849 he founded a congregation of preachers, the Missionary Sons of the Immaculate Heart of Mary (Claretians). In 1850 he was named Archbishop of Santiago in Cuba. He returned to Spain in 1857, having been appointed confessor of Queen Isabella II, and again travelled the country preaching on the Eucharist and the Immaculate Heart of Mary. In Spain he established societies to publish and distribute free literature on the Catholic faith, much of which he himself had written. He was forced to leave Spain during the 1868 revolution and he died at the Cistercian monastery at Fontfroide, France, on October 24, 1870. He was canonized by Pope Pius XII in 1950. The prayer of today's Mass recalls his preaching the gospel to many nations.

October 28
Sts. Simon and Jude, Apostles
Feast

In the lists of the apostles found in the New Testament Simon is called "the Zealot" (Matt. 10:4; Mark 3:18; Luke 6:15; Acts 1:13), and is probably so identified as to distinguish him from Simon Peter. That he should be called "the Zealot" may be because he may have, at one time, belonged to the Jewish Zealot party. Jude is called "Judas son of James" by Luke (6:16; Acts 1:13), but is called Thaddaeus by Matthew (10:3) and Mark (3:18), and is said to have been a relative of the Lord (Matt. 13:55; Mark 6:3). It is far from certain where both these apostles preached after Pentecost; some sources claim that Simon preached in Persia and Babylonia, while Jude preached in Palestine and the Near East. Both Simon and Jude were martyred in the first century, and both have been commemorated in Rome on the same day since the ninth century. Jude is also the author of one of the epistles in the New Testament.

+October 31
St. Alphonsus Rodríguez, Religious
Memorial

St. Alphonsus Rodríguez was born in Segovia, Spain, on July 25, 1533. He was a wool merchant by trade, married, and had three children. It was through the death of his wife and children that God chose to lead him to an extraordinary intimate union with Himself. Being a widower he thought of the priesthood, but was told that he was too old to begin studies. He was then about thirty-five years of age. He thus entered the Jesuits as a coadjutor brother in 1571, and later that year was sent to the College of Montesión in Palma on the island of Mallorca, where he was made doorkeeper and where he remained for the next forty-six years of his life. Externally his life had nothing extraordinary or remarkable about it. He fulfilled his monotonous job with uncommon fidelity, humility, charity, kindness, and obedience, and thus he became a saint. He encouraged the students to have devotion to our Lady and to pray the rosary, and it was he who suggested to Peter Claver (see September 9) to go to the missions in the New World. St. Alphonsus died at Palma on October 31, 1617, and only after his death was it learned how God had favored him with mystical graces, ecstasies, and visions. He was canonized by Pope Leo XIII in 1888. The prayer in the Mass today reminds us that "the way of fidelity" as lived by St. Alphonsus "leads to joy and peace."

November 2
All Souls

In yesterday's Feast of all Saints, we honored the Church in heaven and today we commemorate the Church in purgatory--the deceased who are on their way to heaven. Their present period of purification will infallibly end with their vision of God and union with the saints. This, then, is not a day of mourning, but we rejoice because our faithful departed have been judged worthy to be with God. As early as the seventh century certain monastic communities had specified a day for commemorating the dead of their particular community. This practice spread and by the ninth century it became a commemoration of all the dead. In 998 St. Odilo,

Abbot of Cluny (France), established that in his communities the commemoration of the faithful departed was to be celebrated on November 2. In the fifteenth century the custom arose in Spain of celebrating three Masses for the deceased on November 2, and this custom prevailed throughout Spain, Portugal, and Spanish America. Then in 1915 Pope Benedict XV, alert to the large number of deaths during World War I, which was then raging, extended to the entire Latin Church the privilege of celebrating three Masses for the deceased on this day.

November 3
+Bl. Rupert Mayer, Priest

Bl. Rupert Mayer was born in Stuttgart, Germany, on January 23, 1876. After completing his university studies, he went to the seminary and was ordained a diocesan priest in 1899. The following year he entered the Society of Jesus, and shortly thereafter he traveled through Germany and Switzerland giving parish missions. In 1912 he was assigned to Munich and from then on his name was closely linked with that city. During World War I he volunteered as an army chaplain and served until he was wounded. After the war he was again in Munich. Witnessing the rise of Hitler he spoke out against him and the falsehoods he was propagating, and because he had the courage to oppose the Nazis, he was three times arrested by the Gestapo and three times imprisoned, the last in a concentration camp. He survived the war, was liberated in May 1945, and returned to his beloved Munich. Five months later he died on November 1, 1945. He was beatified by Pope John Paul II in 1987.

Same day
St. Martin de Porres, Religious

St. Martin de Porres was born in Lima, Peru, on December 9, 1579, the son of a Spanish father and a Negro mother. As a youth he learned the basics of medical practice by helping one of the local pharmacist-physicians. He felt called to the religious life, but since he was a mulatto he thought that that way of life was not for him, so when he was fifteen he got a job doing domestic work in a Dominican monastery. During his nine years there the monks witnessed his humility and charity and eventually they asked him if he would not want to become a Dominican brother. This he did in 1603. In addition to his regular tasks in the community Br. Martin cared for the sick and the poor of the city, and when he returned home he spent his nights more in prayer than in sleep. To the people of the city and to his religious brethren he was the living symbol of humility. He died in Lima on November 3, 1639, and was canonized by Pope John XXIII in 1962. Today's prayer mentions St. Martin's humility.

November 4
St. Charles Borromeo, Bishop
Memorial

St. Charles Borromeo, the son of Count Borromeo, was born at Arona in Lombardy, Italy, on October 2, 1538. He studied at the University of Pavia and earned a doctorate in civil and canon law. When his mother's brother was elected pope (Pius IV) in 1559, Charles was called to Rome, and in 1560, when he was only twenty-two, he was made cardinal, named Archbishop of Milan, and head of the Secretariat of State. After his ordination (1563) he lived an austere life, and when his uncle died he made his residence in Milan and from 1566 until his death he was an exemplary bishop. He convoked synods and councils to bring the diocese into line with the prescriptions of the Council of Trent, established seminaries and colleges, built shelters for the homeless and homes for the abandoned, as well as orphanages and hospitals. When Milan suffered from a plague, he cared for the sick and buried the dead without a worry about himself. He died on November 3, 1584. In life the people considered him the ideal pastor and shepherd, and in death they venerated him as a saint. He was canonized by Pope Paul V in 1610. The prayers today recall St. Charles' reforming activity when it prays that the "Church be continually renewed" and speaks of him as "an example of virtue and concern for the pastoral ministry."

+November 5
All Saints and Blessed of the Society of Jesus
Feast

But a few days ago we celebrated the Feast of All Saints, and today we wish to honor those of our Jesuit family who are with God: the canonized saints, the beatified, the countless others who, in following the prescriptions of our Institute, have attained heaven. Holiness is our goal in life, and today's feast tells us that heaven is within our reach. We do not become holy on our own; it is God who is the source of all holiness. As we praise our brethren in heaven for their faithfulness to God while on earth, we take encouragement for we too labor under the same banner of Christ as they did, and since God has called us, weak though we are, to follow Him, may our service be pleasing to Him and may it bring us to the same goal that our brothers in heaven now possess.

November 9
Dedication of St. John Lateran
Feast

The Basilica of St. John Lateran dates from about 324 when Constantine (emperor 306-337) converted a part of the palace of the Laterani into a Christian basilica, and gave the property to Pope Sylvester I to become the papal residence. Since this church was the first in date, and the first in dignity--it became the seat and cathedral of the Bishop of Rome--it is referred to as "The Mother and Head of all Churches, in the City and the World," as the inscription on the church's facade indicates. The actual day of its dedication is unknown, but in the twelfth century the canons who staffed the basilica celebrated the anniversary of its dedication on November 9. The anniversary was first celebrated only in Rome, but then it was extended to the whole Church to indicate the unity between the churches of the world and that of the Chair of Peter. The basilica is now commonly known as that of St. John Lateran: John because it is dedicated to Sts. John the Baptist and John the Evangelist, and Lateran to commemorate the family whose property it once had been.

November 10
St. Leo the Great, Pope and Doctor
Memorial

St. Leo was probably born in Rome about 400. He was a deacon under popes Celestine I (422-432) and Sixtus III (432-440), both of whom had entrusted him with diplomatic missions. He was elected pope in August/September 440, while absent on a mission to Gaul, and was consecrated (September 29, 440) on his return to Rome. Leo is one of the two popes designated as "the Great" and he merits this title because of his teaching and his governance. His teaching is found in ninety-seven sermons which explain the major tenets of the Catholic faith. With regard to governance, he was the best administrator of the ancient Church; he consolidated Church administration and also stressed the primacy of the Roman see in his dealings with the rest of the Church. He likewise urged liturgical (*Leonine Sacramentary*) as well as canonical and pastoral uniformity. Near Mantua he confronted (452) Attila the Hun and persuaded him to withdraw, and on meeting the Vandal Gaiseric outside Rome, he induced (455) him to spare the city from fire and massacre. He died on November 10, 461. Pope Benedict XIV declared him a Doctor of the Church in 1754. Our opening prayer today echoes St. Leo's constant teaching that the Church is founded on the rock of Peter.

November 11
St. Martin of Tours, Bishop
Memorial

St. Martin was born of pagan parents in Sabaria, Pannonia (today's Hungary), about 316. His father was an officer in the Roman army and moved his family to Pavia (Italy), where Martin grew up and became a catechumen. At age fifteen he joined the army and tradition has it that while serving near Amiens (France) he shared his military cloak with a destitute beggar, and afterwards was granted a vision of Christ who, wearing that beggar's cloak, encouraged him to be baptized. After Martin's discharge (356) from military service, he placed himself under the spiritual guidance of St. Hilary of Poitiers (see January 13) and later founded (360/361) a monastery at Ligugé, near Poitiers. This was the first monastery established in Gaul. He was made Bishop of

Tours in 371, but continued his monastic life outside the city. He died on a pastoral visit to Candes on November 8, 397, and was buried in Tours on November 11. His successor in the see built a chapel over his tomb, which soon became a place of pilgrimage. The Communion antiphon in today's Mass was chosen to recall St. Martin's charity in dividing his cloak with the beggar.

November 12
St. Josaphat, Bishop and Martyr
Memorial

St. Josaphat Kuncewycz is known as the "Apostle of Union" because he gave his life to promote union between the Catholic and Orthodox Churches. He was born of Orthodox parents in Vladimir, Ukraine, about 1580, and while working as a merchant in Vilnius (Lithuania), be became a Catholic and then entered (1604) the Order of St. Basil. He was ordained in 1609 and set about preaching to gain adherents to the Union of Brest (union of the Ruthenian Orthodox and Catholic Churches), and since he was successful, he was named (1617) Bishop of Vitebsk (Belorussia), and a bit later became Archbishop of Polotsk (Belorussia). With the appointment of a new Orthodox hierarchy in Lithuania, he not only met opposition, but it was now directed against him. On November 12, 1623, he was attacked by an enraged mob outside the cathedral in Vitebsk and was slain. He was canonized by Pope Pius IX in 1867. The Communion prayer today mentions the unity of the Church for which St. Josaphat gave his life.

November 13
+St. Stanislaus Kostka, Religious
Memorial

St. Stanislaus Kostka was a Polish noble youth born
in 1550 in Mazovia, Poland. When he was fourteen he
was sent (1564) with his brother to study at the Jesuit
college in Vienna. There he had to endure many a trial
at the hands of his brother, but these never diminished
his resolve to live a prayerful and recollected life. When
ill and longing to receive Holy Communion, Stanislaus
enjoyed extraordinary favors from God. His heart was
set on becoming a Jesuit, but knowing that his parents
would not give their consent, he quietly left (August
1567) Vienna and walked 450 miles to Dillingen,
Germany. There he met the Jesuit provincial, St. Peter
Canisius (see April 27), who arranged for him to go to
Rome. When Stanislaus arrived in Rome (October
1567) he was accepted by St. Francis Borgia (see
October 3) and immediately began his novitiate training.
In early August of the following year he had a
premonition that he would die on the 15th of that
month; he became ill on the 10th, and died on August
15, 1568, as he had foretold. He was canonized by Pope
Benedict XIII in 1726. The prayer of today's Mass
speaks of St. Stanislaus' generosity of heart, and hints
that though his was a short life, nevertheless, it was
filled with good works.

Same day
St. Frances Xavier Cabrini, Virgin
Memorial

St. Frances Xavier Cabrini was born at Sant' Angelo
Lodigiano, in Lombardy, in northern Italy, on July 15,
1850. At age eighteen she received her teacher's license

and taught for a few years. She then did charitable work in an orphanage, the House of Providence, and there she joined the Sisters of Providence. When the hospital closed and the sisters disbanded, Frances thought of doing missionary work in a foreign country. During a meeting with Pope Leo XIII she told him that she was unable to find a congregation of sisters who were missionaries. To this the pope replied: "Found your own group!" In 1880, with several companions from the House of Providence, she established the Missionary Sisters of the Sacred Heart. In 1889 she and six of her sisters went to New York and began working among the Italian immigrants. They started schools, hospitals, orphanages, and taught catechism to children. Wherever there was an Italian community, the sisters went to serve them. Frances died in Chicago on December 22, 1917, and was canonized by Pope Pius XII in 1946. The prayer in today's Mass speaks of St. Frances' leaving Italy to work with the immigrants and how, in her charity, she cared for the sick and the frustrated.

+November 14
St. Joseph Pignatelli, Priest
Memorial

St. Joseph Pignatelli was born of noble parents in Saragossa, Spain, on December 27, 1737. He entered the Jesuits in 1753, and was ordained in 1762. When King Charles III of Spain expelled the Jesuits from his kingdom in 1767, they were deported to Italy, where they settled as best they could. With the Society's suppression in 1773, the Jesuits took on tasks in the various dioceses, but Fr. Pignatelli kept in contact with them, looking ahead to the time when they could all be reunited. Since the Jesuits were never suppressed in the territory of Catherine the Great of Russia, Fr. Pignatelli associated himself with them but remained and worked in Italy. He lived in exile for forty years, regrouping the former Jesuits, and awaiting the day when the Society could be restored throughout the world. He was not to see that day, for he died on November 15, 1811, three years prior to the Society's restoration by Pope Pius VII in 1814. He was canonized by Pope Pius XII in 1954. The opening prayer in the Mass today refers to St. Joseph Pignatelli's "courage and strength" in uniting "his scattered brethren."

November 15
St. Albert the Great, Bishop and Doctor

St. Albert the Great was an eminent scientist, philosopher, and theologian and is called "the Great" because of his immense erudition. He was born in Lauingen, near Ulm, Germany, about 1200. He entered the Dominicans in 1223, and after ordination taught theology. In 1241 he went to the University of Paris where he earned his degree and later lectured (1245-1248). He then taught at Cologne, Germany, and subsequently became provincial (1253-1257) of the German Dominicans. In 1260 he was named Bishop of Regensburg, but he resigned two years later to return to teaching and writing. Even during his lifetime he was regarded as a man superior in every branch of learning and was called the wonder and miracle of his age. In recognition of his theological expertise, he was invited to attend the Council of Lyons (1274). He died in Cologne on November 15, 1280, and Pope Pius XI canonized (1931) him and declared him a Doctor of the Church. Today's opening prayer mentions that in St. Albert human wisdom and divine faith were combined, and prays that the advance in human knowledge deepen our love of God.

November 16
+Sts. Roch González, Priest, and Companions, Martyrs
Memorial

St. Roch González was born in Asunción (Paraguay) in 1576, was ordained a diocesan priest, and later entered (1609) the Society of Jesus. He was first assigned to evangelize the Indians, and then placed in charge of various reductions along the River Plate, where he supervised the construction of houses for the Indians and founded schools and built churches. While teaching the Indians the essentials of farming, he also taught them the fundamentals of the Catholic faith. In time the reductions in Paraguay became ideal Christian communities. Because of his success in peacefully bringing the Indians together and christianizing them, a local witch doctor, seeing that his own influence was lessening, decided that the missionaries had to die. On November 15, 1628, Fr. González was in Caaró (in today's Brazil), and as he left chapel after celebrating Mass, the witch doctor and his henchman attacked him and another Jesuit, Fr. Alphonsus Rodríguez, a Spaniard, and martyred them. Two days later the murderers went to the reduction at Iyuí and there they killed another Spanish Jesuit, Fr. John del Castillo. The three martyrs were canonized by Pope John Paul II in 1988. When today's prayer speaks of "a hundredfold in a harvest of justice and peace" it summarizes what St. Roch González and his companions were trying to accomplish in the Jesuit reductions of South America.

Same day
St. Margaret of Scotland

St. Margaret, the daughter of the Anglo-Saxon Prince Edward Atheling and Princess Agatha of Hungary, was born in Hungary in 1046, but was brought up in England at the court of her great-uncle Edward the Confessor. After the Battle of Hastings, she attempted (1067) to return to Hungary, but was shipwrecked off the coast of Scotland. There she married (1070) Malcolm III, King of Scotland, and bore him eight children. Together with her husband she initiated a series of reforms that changed the religious life of Scotland. She restored churches and founded (about 1074) the Abbey at Dunfermline, but Queen Margaret was especially known for her goodness and love toward the poor and the sick. She died in Edinburgh on November 16, 1093, was buried in the Abbey church at Dunfermline, and was canonized by Pope Innocent IV in 1250. The opening prayer of today's Mass speaks of St. Margaret's special love for the poor and describes her as a living sign of God's goodness.

Same day
St. Gertrude, Virgin

St. Gertrude was born on January 6, 1256, and when she was five she was entrusted to the care of the Cistercian nuns at Helfta in Thuringia. There she was educated and entered the monastery. When she was twenty-five (1281) she underwent a mystical experience that she called her "conversion," and from that time onward she lived a life of contemplation rich in extraordinary mystical experiences. The monastic liturgy served as the source for her spiritual life; she was also one of the first to promote devotion to the Sacred Heart. She died at Helfta on November 17, 1301 or 1302. Her cult was first authorized in 1606 and then extended to the entire Church by Pope Clement XII in 1738.

November 17
St. Elizabeth of Hungary, Religious
Memorial

St. Elizabeth, the daughter of King Andrew II of Hungary, was born in 1207. The following year she was betrothed to the son of the Landgrave of Thuringia (Germany), and when she was four (1211) she was sent there to be raised according to the customs of that country. At fourteen (1221), she was married to Louis IV, now Landgrave, and bore three children. Besides being wife and mother, she gave of herself and of her wealth to serve God by relieving the needs of the poor. After her husband's death during the crusade of 1227, she provided for her children, gave up her possessions, and took (March 1228) the habit of the Third Order of St. Francis. She then built a hospital in Marburg, where she herself nursed the sick and cared for the poor. She died during the night of 16-17 November, 1231, at age twenty-four. Four years after her death she was canonized (1235) by Pope Gregory IX. The prayer in the Mass today recalls St. Elizabeth's honoring "Christ in the poor of this world."

November 18
Dedication of the Churches of
Sts. Peter and Paul, Apostles

Over the tombs of the Apostles Peter and Paul in
Rome, Constantine (emperor 306-337) built two
basilicas. That over St. Peter's tomb on Vatican Hill
was built about 324 and was dedicated about 326. That
over St. Paul's tomb on the Ostian Way was built about
the same time, but since it proved too small to hold all
the pilgrims that visited it, it was rebuilt and dedicated
again in 390. By the eleventh century the dedication of
St. Peter's was celebrated annually on November 18, and
in the following century this commemoration also
included that of St. Paul's. This celebration, however,
remained a local feast for Rome until 1568 when Pope
Pius V placed it in the Roman Calendar. When St.
Peter's had to be rebuilt in the sixteenth and seventeenth
centuries, Pope Urban VIII dedicated the new basilica
on November 18, 1626. St. Paul's was likewise rebuilt,
due to a fire in 1823, and it was again dedicated by Pius
IX on December 10, 1854. By commemorating the
dedication of these churches of Sts. Peter and Paul in
Rome, we honor the princes of the apostles, and in
today's prayer we ask that the Church always enjoy "the
protection of the apostles" since "it first received the
faith of Christ" through them.

Same day
St. Philippine Duchesne, Virgin

St. Philippine Duchesne, was an intrepid pioneer
and persevering missionary. She was born in Grenoble,
France, on August 29, 1769, and despite her father's
opposition, she entered (1788) the Visitation convent of
Sainte-Marie-d'en-Haut. Later, because of the French

Revolution, the community was dispersed (1792) and, thus, she returned home and spent her time teaching neglected children and caring for the sick. When peace returned she purchased (1801) the convent building from the government and tried to bring the Visitation Sisters together again, but this proved impossible. Having heard of a new congregation, the Sisters of the Sacred Heart, she offered (1804) herself and the building to the foundress, St. Madeleine Sophie Barat. Then in 1818 her dream of missionary work in the New World came true. Bishop Du Bourg of the Louisiana Territory requested sisters to teach Indian and French children in his diocese. Mother Philippine asked to go and she and four companions landed in New Orleans in May 1818. They made their way to St. Louis, and that September she opened at St. Charles, near St. Louis, the first free school for girls west of the Mississippi. Life on the frontier was far from easy; they lived and taught in unheated log cabins. In succeeding years more schools were opened; parish schools, schools for Indian girls and schools for boarding students. In 1840, when Mother Philippine was in her seventies, she was sent to help start a school among the Potawatomi Indians in Sugar Creek, Kansas. She did not teach--she was never able to learn their language--but she cared for their sick. The Indians called her "Woman-Who-Prays-Always." In 1842 she was recalled to St. Charles and there she died on November 18, 1852. She was canonized by Pope John Paul II in 1988.

November 21
Presentation of Mary
Memorial

The Eastern Church celebrated a feast commemorating Mary's entrance into the Temple in conjunction with the anniversary of the dedication (November 21, 543) of a new basilica in honor of Mary built near the Temple in Jerusalem. In time the feast became known as "the Presentation of Mary in the Temple," recalling an incident not found in the four canonical Gospels but described in other early writings known as apocryphal gospels. According to this tradition, the parents of Mary, Ann and Joachim, presented their three-year-old daughter to God in the Temple, where she was then reared and educated with other girls under the tutelage of holy women. The French knight, Philippe de Mezières, learned of this feast on a visit to Cyprus, and when he returned to France he promoted its celebration. When Pope Gregory XI, then residing in Avignon, heard of it, he introduced it at Avignon in 1372, and Sixtus V later (1585) extended its celebration to the universal Church.

November 22
St. Cecilia, Virgin and Martyr
Memorial

St. Cecilia was one of the most venerated martyrs of the early Church in Rome, and by the end of the fourth or the beginning of the fifth century, a church in the Trastevere section of Rome had been named in her honor. As early as 545 her feast was celebrated there on November 22. That a maid named Cecilia was martyred and buried in the cemetery of Callistus is certain. Nothing else, however, is known about Cecilia except what is found in a life written some two centuries after her death and, hence, not quite reliable. Legend has it that Cecilia was a young Roman maid who had been condemned for her Christian beliefs and ordered to be suffocated in an exceedingly hot steam bath in her home. Since she remained unharmed, she was to be beheaded. She endured three strokes of the sword and died three days later. In 821 Pope Paschal I had her body transferred from the cemetery to her church, which is still one of the favorite churches in Rome.

November 23
+Bl. Miguel Pro, Priest and Martyr

Bl. Miguel Pro was a Mexican, born in Guadalupe de Zacatecas on January 13, 1891. He became a Jesuit in 1911, but because of political upheavals and growing anti-Catholicism in his country, he and other young Jesuit students had to leave (1914) their homeland. He continued his studies in California before going to Spain and Belgium for further studies leading to the priesthood. Though the Catholic Church in Mexico was suffering a most severe persecution under an atheistic government, Fr. Pro returned to Mexico City in July 1926. Catholic priests were hunted as criminals, nevertheless, he carried on his priestly ministry in secret. Since churches were closed, he set up Communion stations in various parts of the city, where the people gathered once a week and to whom he regularly brought Holy Communion. He was arrested on November 18, 1927, and on the morning of November 23, he was led out into the prison yard--in his right hand he grasped his crucifix and in his left his rosary. He looked around and saw rifles pointing at him. Having refused the blindfold, he stretched out his arms in the form of a cross, and when the order to shoot was given, his last prayer before martyrdom was "Viva Cristo Rey!" "Long live Christ the King!" He was beatified by Pope John Paul II in 1988.

Same Day
St. Clement I, Pope and Martyr

St. Clement was the third pope (about 91-101) after St. Peter. Besides the fact that he was pope, the only other thing known about him with certainty is that he wrote (about 96) an epistle to the Church in Corinth, where dissensions had broken out. Pope Clement's epistle is the most important first-century Christian document outside the New Testament. So revered was his letter that in some places it was read in Church and treated as a part of the New Testament itself. Tradition has it that he was exiled by Trajan (emperor 98-107) to the Crimea, where he was forced to work in the quarries. He was later thrown into the sea and drowned. He has always been revered as a martyr.

Same day
St. Columban, Abbot

St. Columban was born at Leinster, Ireland, about 543. He entered the monastery at Bangor, and after teaching in the monastery school for some thirty years, was sent in 591, with twelve companions, to do missionary work on the European continent. They went to Gaul (today's France) and preached to the pagans; Columban eventually settled in Burgundy and there founded three monasteries. When expelled (610) from Burgundy because he had reproved King Theoderic II for his loose morals, Columban went and preached in the vicinity of Zurich (Switzerland), but he was also driven out (612) from there because he opposed the people's pagan practices. He then went to Bobbio (Italy), and in a valley of the Apennines he founded a monastery that became, in time, a famous center of learning. St. Columban died at Bobbio on November

23, 615, and is regarded as the greatest of the Irish missionary monks.

+November 26
St. John Berchmans, Religious
Memorial

St. John Berchmans was born at Diest, Belgium, on March 13, 1599, and attended the Jesuit college in Mechlin, and thus decided to become (1616) a Jesuit. He was then sent (1618) to Rome to the famous Roman College, but in applying himself to his studies he so weakened his health that he fell ill and died on August 13, 1621. Extraordinary accomplishments are not required for holiness, and there was nothing extraordinary in John's short life. It was his ordinary deeds done extraordinarily well that brought him to sanctity. The Jesuits in Rome were convinced that he was a saint and immediately after his death they began collecting data for his canonization. Pope Leo XIII canonized him in 1888. Since St. John Berchmans saw God's will in every little facet of daily living, the prayer today refers to him as "a cheerful giver" who was "always eager to seek [God] and to do [His] will."

November 30
St. Andrew, Apostle
Feast

St. Andrew was a Galilean, born in Bethsaida (John 1:44) and a fisherman by trade (Mark 1:16). He was a disciple of John the Baptist, and it was John who first pointed out the Lord to him (John 1:35-36). After Andrew had met the Lord and talked to Him, he introduced his brother, Simon Peter, to the Lord as well

(John 1:40-42). Andrew and Peter became disciples when the Lord saw them casting their nets into the sea of Galilee, and said to them "Come after me," as today's Gospel (Matt. 4:18-22) narrates. It is said that after Pentecost Andrew preached the gospel in northern Greece, Epirus, and Scythia, and tradition has it that he was crucified at Patras in Greece. After hanging on the cross for two days, he died on November 30, about the year 70. Devotion to St. Andrew spread in the East and his feast was celebrated in Rome during the pontificate of Pope Simplicius (468-483), who converted a building on Rome's Esquiline Hill into a church honoring him. St. Andrew is the patron of Scotland and of Russia.

+December 1
Sts. Edmund Campion, Robert Southwell, Priests, and Companions, Martyrs
Memorial

Today we commemorate the ten canonized and eighteen beatified Jesuit martyrs of England and Wales. All were martyred on their native soil between the years 1581-1679, at a time when the Church was the object of fierce persecution.

St. Edmund Campion was born in London on June 25, 1540, and taught at Oxford University. After becoming a Catholic he entered (1573) the Society of Jesus, and was one of the first Jesuits to be assigned (1580) to the English Mission. England, at the time of his arrival, was a land where the Mass was prohibited and priests were hunted as traitors. Fr. Campion secretly ministered to English Catholics for a year, and then was apprehended on July 16, 1581, and imprisoned. Because he refused to apostatize and accept the religion established by Queen Elizabeth I, he was hanged, drawn and quartered on December 1, 1581.

St. Robert Southwell, one of England's better poets, was born in Norfolk in 1561. He became a Jesuit in Rome in 1578, and returned to England as a missionary in 1586. He secretly labored among the English Catholics for six years, until he was betrayed in June 1592. He suffered imprisonment for two and a half years, during which time he was brutally tortured. He was condemned to death because he was a priest, and was hanged, drawn and quartered on February 21, 1595.

The ten saints commemorated today were canonized by Pope Paul VI in 1970; of the eighteen blessed, three were beatified in 1886, thirteen in 1929, and two in 1987.

Saints

	Birth	Death
Edmund Campion	1540	December 1, 1581
Alexander Briant	1553	December 1, 1581
Robert Southwell	1561	February 21, 1595
Henry Walpole	1558	April 7, 1595
Nicholas Owen	?	March 2, 1606
Thomas Garnet	1575	June 23, 1608
Edmund Arrowsmith	1585	August 28, 1628
Henry Morse	1595	February 1, 1645
Philip Evans	1645	July 22, 1679
David Lewis	1616	August 27, 1679

Blessed

	Birth	Death
Thomas Woodhouse	1535	June 19, 1573
John Nelson	1535	February 3, 1578
Thomas Cottam	1549	May 30, 1582
John Cornelius	1557	July 4, 1594
Roger Filcock	1570 ca.	February 27, 1601
Robert Middleton	1570	April 3, 1601
Francis Page	?	April 20, 1602
Ralph Ashley	?	April 7, 1606
Edward Oldcorne	1561	April 7, 1606

Thomas Holland	1600	December 12, 1642
Ralph Corby	1598	September 7, 1644
Peter Wright	1603	May 19, 1651
William Ireland	1636	January 24, 1679
John Fenwick	1628	June 20, 1679
John Gavan	1640	June 20, 1679
William Harcourt	1609	June 20, 1679
Anthony Turner	1628	June 20, 1679
Thomas Whitbread	1618	June 20, 1679

December 3
St. Francis Xavier, Priest
+Feast

St. Francis Xavier was, perhaps, the greatest missionary since the time of the apostles. He was born in Navarre, Spain, on April 7, 1506, and studied at the University of Paris, where he met (1529) St. Ignatius of Loyola (see July 31) and joined his group. He sailed for India in 1541, and once arrived, he preached to the pearlfishers on India's Fishery Coast, and then began his missionary journeys, preaching and baptizing. After he started a mission, he left it for others to continue, while he himself went to new areas or lands. From India he went to Malaya, then to the Moluccas, and in 1549 he landed in Japan, the first missionary to enter that country. When he later heard about China, he also wanted to go there, and in September 1552 he was on the island of Sancian, off the coast of China, trying to arrange passage to the mainland. There he fell ill and died on December 3, 1552. He was canonized by Pope Gregory XV in 1622 and in 1927 he was made patron of the missions. He was not the first missionary to go to the East, but he was the first to meet with success in establishing permanent Christian communities. Today's prayer hints at his success when it says that God "opened a door in the East" when He sent St. Francis Xavier to preach the Gospel.

December 4
St. John Damascene, Priest and Doctor

St. John Damascene was born in Damascus (Syria) of Arab-Christian parents about the year 645. After his schooling, he gained a position in the caliph's court, but when the caliph showed hostility toward Christians, he resigned (about 700) and went to the Holy Land. There he became a monk in the monastery of St. Saba, near Jerusalem, and was ordained. He taught in the monastery, preached in Jerusalem, and spent most of his time writing. When Iconoclasm arose in the East, he vigorously opposed it, supported the veneration of images and in his writings offered theological arguments for his position. He died on December 6, about 750. Shortly after his death, he was condemned (754) by an iconoclastic council, but the Second Council of Nicaea officially approved (787) his teaching. Of all his writings, the most important is his *Exposition of the Orthodox Faith*, which is a synthesis of the teaching of earlier Fathers on the principal themes of the Christian faith. By the end of the eighth century he was honored as a saint, and Pope Leo XIII declared him a Doctor of the Church in 1890. When today's prayer mentions "the true faith he taught so well," this is a reference to St. John Damascene's writings.

December 6
St. Nicholas, Bishop

St. Nicholas has always been one of the most popular saints in Europe, nonetheless, the only certain fact we know of his life is that he was Bishop of Myra in ancient Lycia (now modern Turkey) during the first half of the fourth century. Tradition has it that he was born in Patara (Lycia) about 270 and that he died on December 6, between 345 and 352. Justinian I (emperor 526-565) built a church in his honor in the early sixth century. In 1087 Italian soldiers stole the saint's body from Myra and transported it by sea to Bari (Italy), and since then his cult quickly spread through Italy and Europe. Numerous legends arose about his charity and liberality, the most famous is his secretly providing dowries for three poor girls. Based on this legend St. Nicholas became the secret bringer, on the eve of his feast, of presents to children. And in English speaking countries, St. Nicholas has become Santa Claus, the bringer of gifts to children on Christmas Eve.

December 7
St. Ambrose, Bishop and Doctor
Memorial

St. Ambrose was born of an aristocratic Roman family in Trier (Germany), about 340. His father was prefect of Gaul, and after his father's death, the family returned to Rome where Ambrose studied (361-365) law. In 365 he entered civil service and in 370 he was named governor of Liguria and Aemilia, with residence in Milan (Italy). As governor he gained a reputation for uprightness and blameless character. When the bishop died, and when a suitable successor could not be found, Ambrose, though still a catechumen, was unanimously chosen as Bishop of Milan. He was baptized, ordained, and then consecrated bishop on December 7, 374. He immediately began to study theology and set an example of austerity. As bishop he championed orthodoxy against the Arians, was a staunch advocate of the rights of the Church, and an exemplary pastor of souls. It was by hearing Ambrose's sermons that Augustine was converted and baptized in Milan in 387. Ambrose wrote many important dogmatic, exegetical, moral, and ascetical works, and in recognition of these he is honored as one of the four great Doctors of the Western Church. He likewise wrote several Latin hymns which are still in use. He died on Holy Saturday, April 4, 397. His feast is celebrated on the anniversary of his episcopal consecration.

December 11
St. Damasus I, Pope

St. Damasus was a Roman, born about 305; he was a deacon under Pope Liberius (352-366), and accompanied him when the pope had to go into exile in 355. When Pope Liberius died, Damasus was elected his successor and was consecrated on October 1, 366. As pope Damasus opposed heresies (Arianism, Apollinarianism) and carried out liturgical reforms. He was the first pope to call the See of Rome the Apostolic See, and it was during his pontificate that Latin became the principal liturgical language in Rome. He commissioned St. Jerome (see September 30) to revise the Latin translation of the New Testament, promoted the cult of the martyrs, preserved their tombs in the catacombs, and wrote Latin inscriptions for them. He died in Rome on December 11, 384. Today's prayer reminds us that "St. Damasus loved and honored [the] martyrs."

December 12
Our Lady of Guadalupe
Feast

The shrine of Our Lady of Guadalupe, on the outskirts of Mexico City, is undoubtedly the most famous shrine of our Lady in the Western Hemisphere, and today we commemorate her appearances to an Indian convert, Juan Diego, on Tepeyac hill. On December 9, 1531, our Lady appeared to Juan and asked that a church be built on that spot, and on December 12, she again appeared to him and urged him to take her message to the bishop. To offer proof that he was our Lady's messenger, she told Juan to gather the flowers he found blooming there in mid-December. When Juan stood before the bishop, he opened his cloak and as the flowers cascaded to the floor, they saw on the rough cloth an image of our Lady. That is the image still preserved in the shrine. In 1754, Pope Benedict XIV set December 12 as the feast of Our Lady of Guadalupe, and in 1945, when Pope Pius XII was speaking of her, he called her "Queen of Mexico and Empress of the Americas" and went on to say that the image on the cloak was done "by brushes that were not of this world." The prayer in the Mass today affirms that by the Virgin Mary's appearance at Tepeyac God has blessed the Americas.

December 13
St. Lucy, Virgin and Martyr
Memorial

St. Lucy was martyred in Syracuse, Sicily, about 304, during the persecution under Diocletian (emperor 284-305). Devotion to her in Sicily was popular in the fifth century, and from there it spread to northern Italy during the following centuries. Her name is found in the Roman Canon, and it was probably placed there by Pope Gregory I (590-604). Whatever else is said about St. Lucy is derived from an account of her death written three centuries later and, hence, of questionable reliability. The name "Lucy" means "light," and this is most probably why she had been invoked during the Middles Ages in cases of eye-disease, and is often portrayed with eyes on a plate. She is still a popular saint in Italy and Spanish-speaking countries.

December 14
St. John of the Cross, Priest and Doctor
Memorial

St. John's family name was Yepes and he was born of poor parents in Fontiveros, Spain, on June 24, 1542. In 1563 he entered the Carmelite Order, then studied at Salamanca, and was ordained in 1567. Soon after ordination he met St. Teresa of Jesus (see October 15), who told him that she and her religious sisters were following the primitive Carmelite Rule. Since John was then searching for a more austere form of religious life, he adopted St. Teresa's reform and started (1568) a monastery of his own. It was at this time that he changed his name to John of the Cross. His reformed group soon grew in numbers, but since some of the other Carmelites wanted to put a stop to this expansion, they seized (1577) him and imprisoned him. He escaped (August 1578) after ten months of imprisonment and returned to his monastery. For the remainder of his life John of the Cross guided his monasteries and wrote ascetical treatises. He is especially renowned for his mystical poetry and his ascetical writings. He died in Ubeda, Spain, on December 14, 1591, and was canonized by Pope Benedict XIII in 1726. Recognizing the influence that St. John of the Cross' mystical writings had in the Church, Pope Pius XI declared him a Doctor of the Church in 1926.

December 23
St. John of Kanty, Priest

St. John, whose family name was Wacienga, was born in Kanty, in the diocese of Cracow, Poland, on June 23, 1390. He studied at the Cracow Academy, earned a master's degree, and was ordained (1416) a priest. For a time he was rector (1421-1429) of the Templars' school at Miechów, but then returned to the Academy to teach philosophy. In 1443 he received his doctorate in theology, and lectured on that subject at the Academy. He was a devoted and conscientious professor, but he had a greater reputation for sanctity than for brilliance in lecturing. Throughout his life he was always generous and compassionate to the poor. He died in Cracow on Christmas Eve, December 24, 1473, and was buried in the church near the Academy where he had taught. He was canonized by Pope Clement XIII in 1767. When today's opening prayer speaks of "understanding and kindness to others," it reflects St. John's charity and interest in the poor.

December 26
St. Stephen, First Martyr
Feast

According to the New Testament accounts, St. Stephen was the first to give his life in witness for his faith in Christ. The Church, from its earliest days, judged that the commemoration of its first martyr should be on the first day after the celebration of

Christ's birth. When the apostles decided that there was need for deacons in the Church, Stephen was the first of seven chosen, and he was said to have been "filled with faith and the Holy Spirit" (Acts 6:5-6). As a result of his preaching, he was falsely accused and arrested (Acts 6:12-14); he was then dragged out of the city and stoned to death (Acts 7:54-59), as the first reading in today's Mass relates. Stephen's cult quickly took hold in the East and the early *Martyrology of Nicomedia* (360) gives his feast as December 26. When today's opening prayer says that St. Stephen prayed "for those who killed him," this is a reference to his final words, "Lord, do not hold this sin against them" (Acts 7:60).

December 27
St. John, Apostle and Evangelist
Feast

St. John was a Galilean, a son of Zebedee and the brother of James (Matt. 4:21); his mother was probably Salome (Mark 15:40 and Matt. 27:56), who may have been the sister of our Lady (John 19:25). John was a fisherman by trade, and he and his brother James were with Simon (Luke 5:10) when they were called from their nets and boats to follow Christ (Matt. 4:21-22). During John's years with the Lord, he was privileged to witness the raising of Jairus' daughter (Mark 5:37), our Lord's transfiguration (Mark 9:2), and His agony in the Garden of Gethsemane (Mark 14:33). It was John who stood at Jesus' cross and it was to him that our Lord entrusted His mother (John 19:26-27). John likewise went with Peter to the tomb on the first Easter morning and found it empty, as today's Gospel reading (John 20:2-8) narrates. Besides being one of the twelve apostles John is also an evangelist. After Pentecost he settled in Ephesus, but at the time of Domitian (emperor 81-96) he was exiled to the island of Patmos and there he wrote the Book of Revelation (Rev. 1:9). He subsequently returned to Ephesus under Nerva (emperor 96-98) and there, in his old age, wrote his Gospel and three epistles. John died at Ephesus about the year 100. The prayers in the Mass today recall that through his Gospel St. John has passed on to us the "mysteries of the Word" that God had revealed to him. Of the four evangelists, John is the only one who refers to Jesus as "Word" (John 1:1-14).

December 28
Holy Innocents, Martyrs
Feast

The Jewish historian Flavius Josephus (37-100) considered King Herod (73-4 B.C.) to have been a "man of great barbarity." Even if Herod had not slain other individuals, which he did and in great numbers, the slaughter of the Innocents in Bethlehem would admirably prove Josephus' statement. Today's Gospel reading (Matt. 2:13-18) relates how Herod "ordered the massacre of all the boys two-years-old and under in Bethlehem and its environs." The actual number of children killed on that occasion is unknown. In centuries past the number was given in the thousands, even up to 14,000, obviously to emphasize Herod's cruelty. At the time of Christ, however, Bethlehem was but a small town, and judging from the number of people who probably lived there, together with the number of births a year, demographers think that the number of male children massacred might have been between twenty and thirty. Though the number is less, it does not lessen Herod's barbarity. These children were venerated as martyrs as early as the fourth century; martyrs, not because they died for Christ, but because they died in the place of Christ. Their's was, as the prayer after Communion indicates, a "wordless profession of faith" in Christ, and thus they "were crowned with life at his birth."

December 29
St. Thomas Becket, Bishop and Martyr

St. Thomas Becket was born of Norman parents, in London, in 1117 or 1118. After his schooling, he became a member of Archbishop Theobald's staff at Canterbury. In 1154 King Henry II of England made Thomas his chancellor, and both king and chancellor worked together in great harmony. When Archbishop Theobald died, King Henry, looking for someone who would do whatever he wanted, chose (1162) his friend Thomas to succeed as archbishop. Opposition, however, soon arose between king and archbishop; Henry wanted to have complete control of the Church, and Thomas, knowing that his duty was now primarily to God, fought for the freedom and rights of the Church. When Henry moved to have Thomas arrested, Thomas went (1164) into exile in France. When their differences were reconciled, Thomas returned to England during the summer of 1170. But the king immediately returned to his old tricks and Thomas excommunicated him. Henry responded by sending four knights to Canterbury; they found Thomas in his cathedral and there they murdered him on December 29, 1170. Thomas was immediately venerated as a martyr, and countless miracles were reported at his tomb. He was canonized by Pope Alexander III in 1173. St. Thomas Becket's tomb in Canterbury cathedral was a center for pilgrimages until 1538 when King Henry VIII had the saint's tomb dismantled.

Sunday after Christmas or December 30
Holy Family
Feast

When God the Father ordained that his only Son should be born an infant in Bethlehem, he likewise chose that He should be brought up within a human family. In celebrating the feast of the Holy Family, we celebrate the "hidden years" of the life of Mary, Joseph, and Jesus. These years are "hidden" not only because they were lived in out-of-the-way Nazareth, but also because the Gospels are, but for a single incident, silent about them. After their return from Egypt and their going to Nazareth (Matt. 2:19-23), the only incident we know of during this long period is when Mary and Joseph find Jesus among the teachers in the Temple (Luke 2:48-52). In the eyes of the people who lived in Nazareth, their's was an ordinary family--Mary and Joseph did the normal things that parents do. Joseph worked as carpenter and provided for the family; Mary ran the household, doing the necessary everyday chores of a mother. And Jesus was obedient to them; he helped about the house, and after Joseph's death, he took over the carpentry business and provided for his mother. In a way their life was no less humdrum than our own, nevertheless, the Holy Family is the model for all Christian families. A model because Mary, Joseph, and Jesus were faithful in their devotion to and love for each other, and thus they lived their lives in peace and harmony.

December 31
St. Sylvester I, Pope

When St. Sylvester, a Roman by birth, became pope on 31 January 314, Constantine was emperor (306-337).

In the previous year (313), Constantine, by the Edict of Milan, had officially recognized the Catholic Church and brought all persecution against the Church to an end. The emperor was favorable to Christianity, but he himself postponed his baptism until he was on his deathbed. It was during Sylvester's peaceful pontificate that the Church had its first rapid growth, and that the basilicas over the tombs of Sts. Peter and Paul were built by Constantine. It was also Sylvester who received from the emperor the property (Lateran) that became the official residence of the popes until the Middle Ages. Though the pope did not attend the Council of Nicaea (325), called by Constantine, he sent representatives to it. Because his pontificate coincided with the years when Constantine was emperor, countless legends arose regarding pope and emperor, such as the pope's curing the emperor from leprosy. These, however, are no more than stories. Sylvester died on December 31, 335, and was buried in the cemetery of Priscilla on Rome's Salarian Way.

Index

DATE DUE